Curiosities of Human Nature

ZERAH COLBURN.

AMONG the intellectual prodigies which sometimes appear to excite the wonder and astonishment of mankind, Zerah Colburn was certainly one of the most remarkable. He was born at Cabot, Vermont, Sept. 1st, 1804. He was the sixth child of his parents, who were persons in low circumstances and of little education. He was regarded as the most backward of the children till he was about six years old, when he suddenly attracted attention by the display of his astonishing powers.

In August, 1810, when his father, Abia Colburn, was one day employed at a joiner's work-bench, Zerah was on the floor, playing among the chips; suddenly, he began to say to himself,—5 times 7 are 35—6 times 8 are 48, &c. His father's attention was immediately arrested by hearing this, so unexpected in a child so young, and who had hitherto possessed no advantages, except perhaps six weeks' attendance at the district school, that summer. He therefore left his work, and turning to the child, began to examine him in the multiplication table. He thought it possible that Zerah had learnt this from the other boys; but finding him perfect in the table, his attention was more deeply fixed, and he asked the product of 13×97, to which 1261 was instantly given as the answer. He now concluded that something unusual had actually taken place; indeed, he has often said he should not have been more surprised if some one had risen up out of the earth and stood erect before him.

It was not long before a neighbor rode up, and stopping at the house, was informed of the singular occurrence. He desired to be a witness of the fact. Zerah was called, and the result of the examination astonished every one present. The strange phenomenon was now rapidly spread throughout the town. Though many were inclined to doubt the correctness of the reports they heard, a personal examination attested their truth. Thus the story originated, which within the short space of a year found its way not only through the United States, but also reached Europe, and extorted expressions of wonder from foreign journals of literature and science in England, France and other countries.

Very soon after the discovery of his remarkable powers, many gentlemen, at that time possessing influence and public confidence throughout the state, being made acquainted with the circumstances, were desirous of having such a course adopted as might most directly lead to a full development of Zerah's talents, and their application to purposes of general utility. Accordingly, it was proposed that Mr. Colburn should carry his son to Danville, to be present during the session of the court. This was done, and the boy was very generally seen and questioned by the judges, members of the bar, and others.

The legislature of Vermont being about to convene at Montpelier, Mr. Colburn was advised to visit that place with his son, which they did in October. Here large numbers had an opportunity of witnessing his calculating powers, and the conclusion was general that such a thing had never been known before. Many questions, which were out of the common limits of arithmetic, were proposed, with a view to puzzle the child, but he answered them correctly; as, for instance,—which is the most, twice twenty-five, or twice five and twenty? Ans. Twice twenty-five. Which is the most, six dozen dozen, or half a dozen dozen? Ans. Six dozen dozen. Somebody asked him how many black beans would make five white ones. Ans. Five, if you skin them! Thus it appeared that the boy could not only compute and combine numbers readily, but that he also possessed a quickness of thought, somewhat uncommon among children, as to other things.

Soon after this, Mr. Colburn took his son to other large towns, and at last to Boston. Here the boy excited the most extraordinary sensation, and several gentlemen of the highest standing proposed to undertake his education. The terms, though very liberal, were not equal to the high-raised expectations of the father. The offer was therefore refused, and Mr. Colburn proceeded to the southern cities, exhibiting his son in public, his performances everywhere exciting the utmost wonder.

The author of these pages had an opportunity of seeing Zerah Colburn, at this period. He was a lively, active boy, of light complexion, his head being rather larger than that of boys generally at his age. He was then six years old, and had the manners common to children of his age. He was playful, even while performing his calculations. The quickness and precision with which he gave answers to arithmetical questions was amazing. Among those proposed to him at Boston, in the autumn of the year 1810, were the following:

What is the number of seconds in 2000 years? The answer, 63,072,000,000, was readily and accurately given. Another question was this: Allowing that a clock strikes 156 times in a day, how many times will it strike in 2000 years? The child promptly replied, 113,800,000 times.

What is the product of 12,225, multiplied by 1,223? Ans. 14,951,175. What is the square of 1,449? Ans. 2,099,601. Suppose I have a corn-field, in which are seven acres, having seventeen rows to each acre, sixty-four hills to each row, eight ears on a hill, and one hundred and fifty kernels on an ear; how many kernels in the corn-field? Ans. 9,139,200.

It will be recollected that the child who answered these questions was but six years old; that he had then had no instruction whatever in arithmetic; that he could neither read nor write, and that he performed these immense calculations by mental processes, wholly his own. His answers were usually given, and the calculations performed, while engaged in his sports, and the longest process seemed hardly to divert his mind from his amusements. His answers were often made almost as soon as the question was proposed, and in most cases before the process could be performed on paper.

His faculty for calculation seemed to increase, and as he became acquainted with arithmetical terms, his performances were still more remarkable. In June, 1811, he was asked the following question: If the distance between Concord and Boston be sixty-five miles, how many steps must I take in going this distance, supposing each step to be three feet? The answer, 114,400 steps, was given in ten seconds. He was asked how many days and hours had elapsed since the Christian era commenced. In twenty seconds he replied, 661,015 days, 15,864,360 hours.

Questions still more difficult were answered with similar promptitude. What sum multiplied by itself will produce 998,001? In less than four seconds he replied 999. How many hours in thirty-eight years, two months, and seven days? The answer, 334,488, was given in six seconds.

These extraordinary performances, witnessed by thousands of people, and among them persons of the highest standing, were soon reported in the papers, and attracted scarcely less attention in Europe than in this country. In England, particularly, great curiosity was expressed, and the plan of taking young Colburn thither was suggested. After some deliberation, this project was resolved upon; and in the spring of 1812, the father and son embarked at Boston for Liverpool, where they landed on the 11th of May. They proceeded to London, and taking rooms at Spring Gardens, commenced their exhibition.

Great numbers came to witness the performances of the boy, among whom Zerah, in his Life, enumerates the dukes of Gloucester and Cumberland, Lord Ashburton, Sir James Mackintosh, Sir Humphrey Davy, and the Princess Charlotte. The latter, attended by her tutor, the bishop of Salisbury, remained a full hour, and asked a number of questions. Among the rest was this: What is the square of 4001? The answer, 16,008,001, was immediately given. The duke of Cambridge asked the number of seconds in the time elapsed since the commencement of the Christian era, 1813 years, 7 months, 27 days. The answer was correctly given, 57,234,384,000.

An extraordinary interest was excited in London in respect to this remarkable youth, and schemes for giving him an education suited to his turn of mind were suggested. At a meeting of several distinguished gentlemen, to mature some plan of this sort, various questions were proposed to the child. He multiplied the number eight by itself, and each product by itself, till he had raised it to the sixteenth power, giving, as the almost inconceivable result, 281,474,976,710,656. He was asked the square root of 106,929, and before the number could be written down, he answered 327. He was then requested to name the cube root of 268,336,125, and with equal facility and promptness he replied, 645.

A likeness of the young prodigy, drawn by Hull and engraved by Meyer, was now published, and sold at a guinea each. Many were sold, and a considerable profit was realized. Another scheme was now started,—a memoir of the child,—and among the committee to superintend its publication, were Sir James Mackintosh, Sir Humphrey Davy and Basil Montague. Several hundred subscribers were obtained, but, though many paid in advance, for some reason or other the work was never published. Young Colburn and his father now made a tour to Ireland and Scotland. Among his visitors in Scotland, were Dugald Stewart, Professor Playfair, Doctor Brewster and Doctor Macknight. In March, 1814, they returned to London. By the advice of friends, they now proceeded to Paris, where they arrived in July, 1814.

Zerah was carefully examined before the French Institute. It is curious that on this occasion he was longer in giving his answers than ever before; probably owing to some embarrassment. His performances, however, excited here, as everywhere else, the greatest astonishment. La Place, the author of the Méchanique Celeste, was present. Guizot received the youth at his house, and expressed in his behalf the liveliest interest.

Such was the feeling excited, that a project was set on foot for giving Zerah an education at the Royal College of Henry IV. Nothing was wanting but the sanction of the king; but at the precise moment when measures were in progress to secure this object, Bonaparte came back from Elba, sweeping everything before him. The Bourbons fled, and the emperor was reinstated upon his throne. Application was now made to him in behalf of young Colburn; his assent was obtained, and on the 13th May, 1815, he entered the seminary, which was now restored to its original title, the Lyceum Napoleon.

Mr. Colburn had, in England, Scotland and Paris, obtained a large number of subscribers to the memoir. Having placed his son in the Lyceum, he went to London to attend to the publication of the work. Here he met with bitter disappointment. His agent, who had been authorized to collect the money, had received about one third of the whole subscriptions, and appropriated the money to his own use. As he was poor, the whole sum was irretrievably lost. At the same time, Mr. Colburn found that his former friends were greatly chagrined to find that the French government, more liberal than themselves, had made provision for his son. Under this influence, the project of the memoir was abandoned, and a new scheme was proposed, the object of which was to raise two hundred pounds a year for six years, to defray the expenses of the boy's education.

While Mr. Colburn was pursuing this scheme, Zerah was at the Lyceum at Paris, which now became the theatre of the most interesting events. The battle of Waterloo was fought, Napoleon fled, and the French army retreated toward the capital. To this point, the hostile armies were now directing their march, and the citizens of Paris were roused for its defence. Every effort was made to strengthen the walls and throw up entrenchments. The scholars at the Lyceum received permission to join in this work, and with enthusiastic ardor, heightened by their sympathy for Napoleon, they went to their tasks, crying, "*Vivel'Emper eur*." Our little mathematician was among the number, and if he could have multiplied forts as easily as he managed figures, Paris would, doubtless, have been saved. But the fortune of war decided otherwise. Paris was overwhelmed, Napoleon dethroned, and Louis XVIII. restored.

Zerah Colburn might have continued at the Lyceum, but his foolish father, having embraced the London scheme, proceeded to Paris, and carried him thence again to London, where they arrived February 7, 1816.

The scheme which had excited Mr. Colburn's hopes, was, however, a mere illusion. His friends were worn out with his importunities, and, doubtless, disgusted with his fickleness. They were dissatisfied by discovering that while he wished to obtain a provision for his son, he desired also that some emolument, sufficient for his own wants, should come to himself. The result was, that both the father and son were reduced to a state of poverty. While attempting, by means scarcely better than beggary, to obtain transient support, they chanced to call upon the Earl of Bristol, who received them kindly, and expressed great interest in the youthful calculator. He invited them to his country residence at Putney, whither they went, and spent several days. The result of this fortunate acquaintance was, that the Earl made a provision of six hundred and twenty dollars a year for young Colburn's education at Westminster school, where he was regularly entered on the 19th September. At this period, he was a few days over twelve years old.

It now seemed that better fortunes had dawned upon this gifted, but still unfortunate boy; but these were soon clouded by disappointment. The custom of fagging existed in this school, as in all the higher seminaries of England. By this system, the boys of the under classes were required to be waiters and servants of those in the upper classes. Zerah was subjected to this arrangement, and a youth in the upper school was pitched upon for his master. This was the son of a baronet, Sir John L. Kaye.

Soon after he had been initiated into these menial duties, one of the upper scholars called upon him to perform some servile task. This he accomplished, but not to the satisfaction of his employer. He therefore complained to young Kaye, his proper master, whose wrath being greatly excited, he fell upon poor Zerah, twisted his arm nearly out of joint, and, placing him in a helpless situation, beat his shoulder black and blue. Zerah went to his father, who immediately proceeded to Mr. Knox, the usher. The latter expressed regret for the abuse Zerah had received, but when the father claimed exemption for his son from the custom of fagging, the usher positively refused compliance. Mr. Colburn enjoined it upon his son by no means to submit to this system of drudgery again, and departed. In the evening, he was called upon to clean a pair of shoes. This he refused; whereupon, a number of the larger boys, who had gathered around him, first threatened, and then beat him without mercy, until at last he complied. All this occurred under the same roof where the usher then was. In the morning, the father came, and appealing to him, was treated with contempt. As he was going across the yard to see Dr. Page, the head master, the boys yelled at him from their windows, calling him Yankee; doubtless, deeming it the most opprobrious of epithets. The final result of this matter was, that Zerah was exempted from the custom of fagging, though no relaxation of the custom, generally, was made in the school.

Zerah continued at Westminster, spending his vacations with the Reverend Mr. Bullen, Lord Bristol's chaplain, at the village of Danton. His father, in the mean time, picked up the means of subsistence, partly by boarding his son and a few other scholars, and partly by contributions. At length, the Earl, who was now in Germany, made an arrangement for the removal of Zerah from the Westminster school to the exclusive charge of Mr. Bullen. Mr. Colburn objected to this, and wrote accordingly to Lord Bristol. The latter persisted in his plan, and in order to reconcile the father to it, offered him fifty pounds a year for his own personal use. With stubbornness, amounting to infatuation, he rejected the generous offer, and withdrew his son from the Westminster school, and the patronage of his noble friend.

Young Colburn had spent two years and nine months at the Westminster seminary, where his progress in the acquisition of languages and other studies was extremely rapid. Euclid's Elements of Geometry were mastered with ease; but it is a curious fact that while the boy was fascinated with arithmetical calculations, as he advanced into the abstruser portions of mathematics, his taste revolted from a pursuit that was dry and repulsive.

Again the father and son were afloat in the sea of London. What was to be done now? The education of his son was, doubtless, an object to Mr. Colburn; but, with blind selfishness, he seems to have thought more of turning him to account as a means of raising money. With this view he proposed that he should go upon the stage; no doubt supposing that the youth's notoriety would render him available in this capacity. He was put in training, under the care of Charles Kemble. After four months' tuition, he appeared at Margate in the character of Norval. His reception was tolerably flattering, but he obtained no compensation. Mr. Colburn now determined to exhibit his son in his new profession, in Scotland and Ireland; but being almost entirely destitute of money, they were obliged to take a steerage passage in a vessel, and subsist upon hard fare. They arrived at Edinburgh, but received no encouragement in the theatrical line. Mr. Colburn called upon his former friends, and they contributed to his immediate relief. They now proceeded by canal-boat to Greenock, and thence in a vessel to Belfast. Here they found a strolling company of players, with whom an arrangement was made for Zerah's appearance at Londonderry, whither the party were about to proceed; to that place father and son journeyed on foot. Here the latter performed in some inferior characters, and soon returned with the band to Belfast. At this place he played the part of Richard the Third—but alas! even this master-stroke of policy failed. The father and son pushed on to Dublin, but they could get no engagement at the theatre.

The inventive resources of Abia Colburn were not yet exhausted. Zerah must now turn author—and the future Methodist preacher must write a play! The subject chosen was that of Tasso's Jerusalem Delivered. The drama was composed—and we believe it was actually performed. But, alas! says Zerah, in his honest, modest book—"it never had any merit or any success."

After an absence of two months, the wanderers returned to London. A long period of inaction follows, during which Zerah wrote plays, which were never printed or performed, and the father picked up a precarious living by levying contributions upon his former friends. These were at last worn out with his importunities, and finally, one of the best of them deliberately turned Zerah out of doors, when he came upon some errand from his father.

Deprived of all other means save that of begging, which was now a poor resource, the youth obtained employment in October, 1821, as an usher in a school, and soon after established one on his own account. This afforded so poor a support, that still another effort was made to raise funds, ostensibly to provide for his permanent relief. To obtain subscribers to this proposal, Zerah went to Edinburgh, Glasgow and Belfast. At the former place, Mr. Combe took a cast of his head, seeking thereby to throw light upon his phrenological theories. He returned to London, with little success, and resumed his school.

The health of his father now began to give way. Unhappily, he had, from the first discovery of his son's extraordinary gifts, looked upon them with mercenary feelings—as a source of revenue. It is true he had a father's love for his child—and in this respect, Zerah, in the simple memoir of his own life, does his parent more than justice; but still, it was this short-sighted selfishness which made him convert his child's endowments into a curse to him, to his friends, and Zerah himself. His expectations had been lifted to such a pitch, that nothing could satisfy them. The most generous offers fell short of what he felt to be his due; liberality was turned, in his mind, to parsimony—and even friends were regarded as little short of enemies. His sanguine temper led him constantly to indulge high hopes, which were as constantly doomed to disappointment. Such a struggle could not always last. His mind was torn with thoughts of his home and family neglected for twelve years; of his life wasted; his prospects defeated; of fond dreams, ending at last in failure, shame and poverty. He failed gradually, and on the 14th February, 1824, he died. A few days after, the body was consigned to the tomb, and Zerah, in his life, notices the fact that John Dunn Hunter was among the mourners. We mention this, as coinciding with the account we have given in this volume of that extraordinary character.

Zerah continued in London for a few months, in the employment of Mr. Young, in making astronomical calculations. He had, however, a desire, enforced by his father's death-bed injunctions, to return to his country, and his mother, at Cabot. Again aided by his friend, Lord Bristol, he was provided with necessary means, and in June, 1824, he arrived at New York. On the third of July he approached his mother's door. He found there an elderly woman, and being uncertain who it was, he asked if she could tell him where the widow Colburn lived. "I am she," was the reply.

The mother of Zerah Colburn was a remarkable woman. During the long absence of her husband, with a family of eight children, and almost entirely destitute of property, she had sustained the burthen with indomitable energy. She wrought with her own hands, in house and field; bargained away the little farm for a better; and, as her son says, "by a course of persevering industry, hard fare, and trials such as few women are accustomed to, she has hitherto succeeded in supporting herself, besides doing a good deal for her children."

Zerah Colburn was now unable to offer much aid to his mother or the family. He found employment for a time as a teacher; but his mind at last was impressed with religious views, and after some vicissitudes of life, and many fluctuations of feeling, he finally adopted the Methodist faith, and became a humble but sincere preacher of that sect. With pious, patient assiduity he continued in this career for a number of years. He published a modest memoir of his life and adventures, from which we have gathered the greater part of our account,—and at last became professor of the Greek, Latin, French and Spanish languages, as well as of classical literature, in the

"Vermont University," at Norwich. At this place he died, March 2d, 1840, in the thirty-eighth year of his age.

Whoever has carefully attended to the facts stated in the early part of this notice, will be prepared to admit that Zerah Colburn was one of the most astonishing intellectual prodigies that has ever appeared. Totally uninstructed in figures, at the age of six years, he was able to perform mental operations which no man living, by all the training of art, is able to accomplish. It had been stated by scientific men, that no rule existed for finding the factors of numbers; yet this child discovered a rule by which he ascertained results of this kind, accessible only to skilful arithmeticians. In the London prospectus, the following facts, in relation to this point, are stated, which cannot fail to excite astonishment.

At one of his exhibitions, among various questions, it was proposed that he should give the factors of 171,395—and he named the following as the only ones: 5×34279; 7×22485; 59×2905; 83×2065; 35×4897; 295×581; 413×415. He was then asked to give the factors of 36,083; but he immediately replied that it had none, which is the fact, it being a prime number. "It had been asserted and maintained by the French mathematicians that 4294967297, was a prime number; but the celebrated Euler detected the error by discovering that it was equal to $641 \times 6,700,417$. The same number was proposed to this child, who found out the factors by the mere operation of his mind."

Great pains were taken to discover the processes by which this boy performed his operations. For a long time he was too ignorant of terms, and too little accustomed to watch the operations of his mind, to do this. He said to a lady, in Boston, who sought to make him disclose his mode of calculation, "I cannot tell you how I do these things. God gave me the power." At a subsequent time, however, while at the house of Mr. Francis Bailey, in London, upon some remark being made, the boy said suddenly, and without being asked—"I will tell you how I extract roots." He then proceeded to tell his operations. This is detailed in Zerah's book; but it in no degree abates our wonder. The rule does not greatly facilitate the operation; it still demands an effort of mind utterly beyond the capacity of most intellects; and after all, the very rule itself was the invention of a child.

As he did not at first know the meaning of the word factor, when desired to find the factors of a particular number, the question was put in this form —"What two numbers multiplied together will produce such a number?" His rule for solving such problems was sought for with much curiosity. At last this was discovered. While in Edinburgh, in 1813, he being then nine years old, he waked up one night, and said suddenly to his father—"I can tell you how I find the factors!" His father rose, obtained a light, and wrote down the rule, at Zerah's dictation.

It appears that when he came to maturity, these faculties did not improve; and after a time he was even less expert in arithmetical calculations than when he was ten years old. It is probable, his whole mind was weakened, rather than strengthened, by the peculiar circumstances of his life. As a preacher, he was in no way distinguished. He says this in his book, with simple honesty; and seems at a loss to understand the design of Providence in bestowing upon him so stupendous a gift, which, so far as he was able to discover, had produced no adequate results.

He suggests, indeed, a single instance, in which an atheist in Vermont, who witnessed his performances in childhood, was induced to reflect upon the almost miraculous powers of the mind, and led to the conclusion that it must have an intelligent author. He saw that which was as hard to believe, as much beyond the routine of experience, as any miracle—and hence fairly concluded that miracles could be true. By this course of reflection he was induced to reject his infidelity, and afterwards became a sincere Christian.

This, we doubt not, was one of the designs of Providence, in the bestowment of Zerah Colburn's wonderful gifts. But their use should not be confined to an individual case. If there is argument for God in a flower, how much more in a child of Zerah Colburn's endowments? What infidelity can withstand such an instance, and still say, there is no God? And farther, let us reflect upon the noble powers of the mind, and rejoice, yet with fear and trembling, that we are possessors of an inheritance, which, at God's bidding, is capable of such mighty expansion.

The history of Zerah Colburn may teach us one thing more—that the gifts of genius are not always sources of happiness to the possessor; that mental affluence, like worldly riches, often brings sorrow, rather than peace to the possessor; and that moderate natural gifts, well cultivated, are generally the most useful in society, and most conducive to the happiness of the possessor.

Zerah Colburn, at eight years of age.

BARATIERE.

JOHN PHILIP BARATIERE was a most extraordinary instance of the early and rapid exertion of mental faculties. He was the son of Francis Baratiere, minister of the French church at Schwoback, near Nuremberg, where he was born, January 10, 1721. The French was his mother tongue, and German was the language of the people around him. His father talked to him in Latin, and with this he became familiar; so that, without knowing the rules of grammar, he, at four years of age, talked French to his mother, Latin to his father, and High Dutch to the servants and neighboring children, without mixing or confounding the respective languages.

About the middle of his fifth year, he acquired a knowledge of the Greek: so that in fifteen months he perfectly understood all the Greek books in the Old and New Testament, which he translated into Latin. When five years and eight months old, he entered upon Hebrew; and in three years more, was so expert in the Hebrew text, that, from a Bible without points, he could give the sense of the original in Latin or French, or translate, extempore, the Latin or French versions into Hebrew. He composed a dictionary of rare and difficult Hebrew words; and about his tenth year, amused himself, for twelve months, with the rabbinical writers.

He now obtained a knowledge of the Chaldaic, Syriac and Arabic; and acquired a taste for divinity and ecclesiastical antiquity, by studying the Greek fathers of the first four ages of the church. In the midst of these occupations, a pair of globes coming into his possession, he could, in eight or ten days, resolve all the problems upon them; and in January, 1735, at the age of fourteen, he devised his project for the discovery of the longitude, which he communicated to the Royal Society of London, and the Royal Academy of Sciences at Berlin!

In June, 1731, he was matriculated in the university of Altorf; and at the close of 1732, he was presented by his father at the meeting of the reformed churches of the circle, at Franconia; who, astonished at his wonderful talents, admitted him to assist in the deliberations of the synod; and, to preserve the memory of so singular an event, it was registered in their acts. In 1734, the Margrave of Brandenburg, Anspach, granted this young scholar a pension of fifty florins; and his father receiving a call to the French church at Stettin, in Pomerania, young Baratiere was, on the journey, admitted master of arts. At Berlin, he was honored with several conversations with the king of Prussia, and was received into the Royal Academy.

Towards the close of his life, he acquired a considerable taste for medals, inscriptions, and antiquities, metaphysical inquiries, and experimental philosophy. He wrote several essays and dissertations; made astronomical remarks and laborious calculations; took great pains towards a history of the heresies of the Anti-Trinitarians, and of the thirty years' war in Germany. His last publication, which appeared in 1740, was on the succession of the bishops of Rome. The final work he engaged in, and for which he had gathered large materials, was Inquiries concerning the Egyptian Antiquities. But the substance of this blazing meteor was now almost exhausted; he was always weak and sickly, and died October 5th, 1740, aged nineteen years, eight months, and sixteen days. Baratiere published eleven different pieces, and left twenty-six manuscripts, on various subjects, the contents of which may be seen in his Life, written by Mr. Formey, professor of philosophy at Berlin.

GASSENDI

Pierre Gassendi, one of the most famous naturalists and philosophers of France, was born at Chantersier, January 22, 1592, of poor parents. They were, however, wise and virtuous people, and perceiving the extraordinary gifts of their son, did everything in their power to promote his education. At the age of four years, young Pierre used to declaim little sermons of his own composition, which were quite interesting. At the age of seven, he would steal away from his parents, and spend a great part of the night in observing the stars. This made his friends say he was born an astronomer. At this age, he had a dispute with some boys, whether it was the moon or the clouds that moved so rapidly; to convince them that it was the latter, he took them behind a tree, and made them take notice that the moon kept its situation between the same leaves, while the clouds passed on.

This early disposition to observation led his parents to place him under the care of the clergyman of the village, who gave him the first elements of learning.

Gassendi and the Boys.

His ardor for study then became extreme: the day was not long enough for him; and he often read a great part of the night by the light of the lamp that was burning in the church of the village, his family being too poor to allow him candles for his nocturnal studies. He often took only four hours sleep in the night. At the age of ten, he harangued his bishop in Latin, who was passing through the village on his visitation; and he did this with such ease and spirit, that the prelate exclaimed—"That lad will, one day or other, be the wonder of his age." The modest and unassuming conduct of Gassendi gave an additional charm to his talents.

In his manners, this remarkable youth was in general silent, never ostentatiously obtruding upon others, either the acuteness of his understanding, or the eloquence of his conversation; he was never in a hurry to give his opinion before he knew that of the persons who were conversing with him. When men of learning introduced themselves to him, he was contented with behaving to them with great civility, and was not anxious to surprise them into admiration. The entire tendency of his studies was to make himself wiser and better; and to have his intention more constantly before his eyes, he had all his books inscribed with these words, *Sapere aude*; "Dare to be wise."

Such was Gassendi's reputation, that at sixteen he was called to teach rhetoric at the seminary of Digne; in 1614, he was made professor of theology in the same institution; and two years after, he was invited to fill the chair of divinity and philosophy at Aix. After passing through various promotions, and publishing several works of great merit on philosophical subjects, Gassendi went at last to Paris, where he gained the friendship of Cardinal Richelieu, and shared the admiration of the learned world with the famous philosopher, Descartes.

Being appointed a professor of mathematics in the College Royal of Paris, he gave his attention to astronomical subjects, and greatly increased his reputation. After a life devoted to science, in which his achievements were wonderful, he died at Paris, October 14, 1655, aged sixty-three years. Distinguished by his vast learning, his admirable clearness of mind, the diversity of his acquirements, the calmness and dignity of his character, and the amiableness of his manners, Gassendi was alike one of the brightest ornaments of his age and of human nature.

PASCAL.

Blaise Pascal "perhaps the most brilliant intellect that ever lighted on this lower world," was born at Clermont, in the province of Auvergne, on the 19th of June, 1623. He was descended from one of the best families in that province. As soon as he was able to speak, he discovered marks of extraordinary capacity. This he evinced, not only by the general pertinency and acuteness of his replies, but also by the questions which he asked concerning the nature of things, and his reasonings upon them, which were much superior to what is common at his age. His mother having died in 1626, his father, who was an excellent scholar and an able mathematician, and who lived in habits of intimacy with several persons of the greatest learning and science at that time in France, determined to take upon himself the whole charge of his son's education.

One of the instances in which young Pascal displayed his disposition to reason upon everything, is the following. He had been told that God rested from his labors on the seventh day, and hallowed it, and had commanded all mankind to suspend their labor and do no work on the Sabbath. When he was about seven years of age, he was seen, of a Sabbath morning, measuring some blades of grass. When asked what he was doing, he replied that he was going to see if the grass grew on Sunday, and if God ceased working on the Sabbath, as he had commanded mankind to do!

Before young Pascal had attained his twelfth year, two circumstances occurred, which deserve to be recorded, as they discovered the turn, and evinced the superiority, of his mind. Having remarked one day, at table, the sound produced by a person accidentally striking an earthenware plate with a knife, and that the vibrations were immediately stopped by putting his hand on the plate, he became anxious to investigate the cause of this phenomenon; he employed himself in making a number of experiments on sound, the results of which he committed to writing, so as to form a little treatise on the subject, which was found very correct and ingenious.

The other occurrence was his first acquisition, or, as it might not be improperly termed, his invention of geometry. His father, though very fond of mathematics, had studiously kept from his son all the means of becoming acquainted with this subject. This he did, partly in conformity to the maxim he had hitherto followed, of keeping his son superior to his task; and partly from an apprehension that a science so engaging, and at the same time so abstracted, and which, on that account, was peculiarly suited to the turn of his son's mind, would probably absorb too much of his attention, and stop the progress of his other studies, if he were at once initiated into it.

But the activity of an inquisitive and penetrating mind is not to be so easily restrained. As, from respect to his father's authority, however, the youth had so far regarded his prohibition as to pursue this study only in private, and at his hours of recreation, he went on for some time undiscovered. But one day, while he was employed in this manner, his father accidentally came into the room, unobserved by Pascal, who was wholly intent on the subject of his investigation. His father stood for some time unperceived, and observed, with the greatest astonishment, that his son was surrounded with geometrical figures, and was then actually employed in finding out the proportion of the angles formed by a triangle, one side of which is produced; which is the subject of the thirty-second proposition in the First Book of Euclid.

The father at length asked his son what he was doing. The latter, surprised and confused to find his father was there, told him he wanted to find out this and that, mentioning the different parts contained in that theorem. His father then asked how he came to inquire about that. He replied, that he had found out such a thing, naming some of the more simple problems; and thus, in reply to different questions, he showed that he had gone on his own investigations, totally unassisted, from the most simple definition in geometry, to Euclid's thirty-second proposition. This, it must be remembered, was when Pascal was but twelve years of age.

His subsequent progress perfectly accorded with this extraordinary display of talent. His father now gave him Euclid's Elements to peruse at his hours of recreation. He read them, and understood them, without any assistance. His progress was so rapid that he was soon admitted to the meetings of a society of which his father, Roberval, and some other celebrated mathematicians were members, and from which afterwards originated the Royal Academy of Sciences, at Paris.

During Pascal's residence with his father at Rouen, and while he was only in his nineteenth year, he invented his famous arithmetical machine, by which all numerical calculations, however complex, can be made by the mechanical operation of its different parts, without any arithmetical skill in the person who uses it. He had a patent for this invention in 1649. His studies, however, began to be interrupted when he reached his eighteenth year by some symptoms of ill health, which were thought to be the effect of intense application, and which never afterwards entirely quitted him; so that he was sometimes accustomed to say, that from the time he was eighteen, he had never passed a day without pain. But Pascal, though out of health, was still Pascal; ever active, ever inquiring, and satisfied only with that for which an adequate reason could be assigned. Having heard of the experiments instituted by Torricelli, to find out the cause of the rise of water in fountains and pumps, and of the mercury in the barometer, he was induced to repeat them, and to make others, to satisfy himself upon the subject.

In 1654, he invented his arithmetical triangle, for the solution of problems respecting the combinations of stakes, in unfinished games of hazard; and long after that, he wrote his Demonstrations of the Problems relating to the Cycloid; besides several pieces on other subjects in the higher branches of the mathematics, for which his genius was probably most fitted. Pascal, though not rich, was independent in his circumstances; and as his peculiar talents, his former habits, and the state of his health, all called for retirement, he adopted a secluded mode of life. From 1655, he associated only with a few friends of the same religious opinions with himself, and lived for the most part in privacy in the society of Port Royal.

At this period, the Catholics being divided into Jesuits and Jansenists, Pascal, being of the latter, published his famous Provincial Letters. These are so distinguished for their admirable wit, their keen argument, and their exquisite beauty of style, as to have even extorted praise from Voltaire and D'Alembert. He also wrote other pieces against the Jesuits, marked with great talent.

Pascal's health, however, continued to decline; and it is probable that his mind suffered in consequence. Though his life had been singularly blameless, still he seemed to be pained with a sense of inward sin. He was accustomed to wear an iron belt around his waist, in which were sharp points, upon which he would strike his elbows, or his arms, when any unholy passion crossed his mind. He continued to practise charity toward all mankind, and severe austerities to himself, until at last he was attacked with sickness, and on the 19th of August, 1662, he died. His last words were, "May God never forsake me!"

The latter part of his life was wholly spent in religious meditations, though he committed to paper such pious thoughts as occurred to him. These were published after his death, under the title of "Thoughts on Religion and other Subjects." They have been greatly admired for their depth, eloquence and Christian spirit.

Pascal.

GROTIUS.

Hugo Grotius, celebrated for his early display of genius and learning, as well as for his adventures and writings in after life, was born at Delft, in Holland, April 10, 1583. He had the best masters to direct his education, and from childhood, was not only distinguished by the great brilliancy of his mind, but also by his application to study. Such was his progress, that, at eight years of age, he composed Latin elegiac verses of great cleverness, and at fourteen, he maintained public theses in mathematics, law, and philosophy with general applause. His reputation by this time was established, and he was mentioned by the principal scholars of the age, as a prodigy of learning, and as destined to make a conspicuous figure in the republic of letters.

In 1598, he accompanied Barnevelt, ambassador extraordinary of the Dutch Republic, in a journey to France, where he was introduced to Henry IV., who was so pleased with his learning, that he presented him with his picture and a gold chain. While in France, he took the degree of doctor of laws. The following year he commenced practice as an advocate, and pleaded his first cause at Delft. In the same year, though then only seventeen, he was chosen historiographer to the United Provinces, in preference to several learned men who were candidates for that office.

Grotius now rapidly rose in rank and reputation: he published several works of great merit, and was appointed to various public offices of high trust. On one occasion he was sent by the government to England to attend to some negotiations, at which time he became acquainted with King James II. But serious religious difficulties now began to agitate Holland. In 1618, a synod met at Dort to take these into consideration. They proceeded to condemn the Arminian doctrines, and to banish all the preachers who upheld them. Barnevelt, who was a celebrated statesman, Grotius, and Hoogurbetz, advocated these sentiments; they were tried and condemned; the first was executed and the two others were sentenced to perpetual imprisonment.

In his prison of Louvestien, Grotius found consolation in literary pursuits. His wife, after much entreaty, was permitted to visit him, and she did everything which the most devoted affection could suggest, to alleviate his confinement. She was accustomed to send him books in the chest which was conveyed out and in, with his linen: this was carefully examined by the jailer, for a time, but finding nothing amiss, he became less suspicious and careful.

Taking notice of this, the wife of Grotius, after he had been confined about two years, devised a scheme for his escape. She pretended to have a large quantity of books to send away. Having a small chest of drawers, about three feet and a half long, she packed her husband into it, and it was carried out by two soldiers, who supposed they were transporting a quantity of books. The chest was now put on a horse, and carried to Gorcum, where the illustrious prisoner was set at liberty.

Disguised in the dress of a mason, with a rule and a trowel in his hand, he fled to Antwerp, which was not under the government of the Stadtholder, Prince Maurice, who had caused his imprisonment. Here he wrote to the State's General of Holland, asserting his innocence of any wrong, in the course he had taken, and for which he had been deprived of liberty. He afterwards went to Paris, where he received a pension from the king.

After the death of Prince Maurice, his confiscated property and estates were restored, and he returned to Holland; but he still found such a spirit of rancor against him, among the principal persons, that he left the country forever, and took up his residence at Hamburgh. Here he received the most flattering proposals from the kings of Portugal, Spain, Denmark, and other countries, who admired his great abilities, and desired him to seek shelter and protection with them.

He finally adopted Sweden as his country, and becoming the queen's ambassador to France, he proceeded, in that character, to Paris, where, for eight years, he sustained the interests of his patron with firmness and dignity. At last, being weary of public life, he solicited his recall. In August, 1648, he embarked for Lubec, where he intended to reside; but, meeting with a dreadful storm, he was driven upon the coast of Pomerania, and obliged to take a land journey of sixty miles, in order to reach Rostock, during which he was exposed to the rain and inclement weather. A fever soon set in, and at midnight, on the 28th of August, the illustrious stranger died.

Grotius has left behind him many works, some of them of great value. His treatise upon the "Truth of the Christian Religion," written in Latin, like his other productions, is one of the best defences of that system which has ever appeared. His work on the law of Peace and War, is still of high authority. We must look upon Grotius as a man of great acuteness, as well as vast expanse of mind. He was, indeed, in advance of his generation, and, like other patriots and philanthropists, who see farther than those around them, he was an object of hatred and disgust, for those very things which in an after age brought him the homage and gratitude of mankind. In an intolerant age, Grotius was in favor of toleration, and this alone was a crime which his generation could not forget or forgive.

NEWTON.

SIR ISAAC NEWTON, the greatest of natural philosophers, was born at Woolsthorpe, in Lincolnshire, December 25, 1642, old style. At his birth he was so small and weak that his life was despaired of. On the death of his father, which took place while he was yet an infant, the manor of Woolsthorpe became his heritage. His mother sent him, at an early age, to the village school, and in his twelfth year, to the seminary of Grantham.

While here he displayed a decided taste for mechanical and philosophical inventions; and avoiding the society of other children, provided himself with a collection of saws, hammers, and other instruments, with which he constructed models of many kinds of machinery. He also made hour-glasses, acting by the descent of water. A new windmill, of a peculiar construction, having been erected in the town, he studied it until he succeeded in imitating it, and placed a mouse inside, which he called the miller.

Some knowledge of drawing being necessary in these operations, he applied himself, without a master, to the study; and the walls of his room were covered with all sorts of designs. After a short period, however, his mother took him home, for the purpose of employing him on the farm and about the affairs of the house. She sent him several times to market, at Grantham, with the produce of the farm. A trusty servant was sent with him, and the young philosopher left him to manage the business, while he himself employed his time in reading. A sundial, which he constructed on the wall of the house at Woolsthorpe, is still shown. His irresistible passion for study and science finally induced his mother to send him back to Grantham. Here he continued for a time, and was entered at Trinity College, Cambridge, 1660.

At the latter place he studied mathematics with the utmost assiduity. In 1667, he obtained a fellowship; in 1669, the mathematical professorship; and in 1671, he became a member of the Royal Society. It was during his abode at Cambridge that he made his three great discoveries, of fluxions, the nature of light and colors, and the laws of gravitation. To the latter of these his attention was first turned by his seeing an apple fall from a tree. The Principia, which unfolded to the world the theory of the universe, was not published till 1687. In that year also Newton was chosen one of the delegates to defend the privileges of the university against James II.; and in 1688 and 1701 he was elected one of the members of the university. He was appointed warden of the mint in 1696; he was made master of it in 1699; was chosen president of the Royal Society in 1703; and was knighted in 1705. He died March 20, 1727.

His "Observations on the Prophecies of Daniel and the Apocalypse" appeared in 1733, in quarto. "It is astonishing," says Dr. Hutton, "what care and industry Newton employed about the papers relating to chronology, church history, &c.; as, on examining them, it appears that many are copies over and over again, often with little or no variation." All the works of this eminent philosopher were published by Dr. Samuel Horsley, in 1779, in five volumes, quarto; and an English translation of his "Philosophæ Naturalis Principia Mathematicæ," is extant.

The character of this great man has been thus drawn by Mr. Hume, in his history of England. "In Newton, Britain may boast of having produced the greatest and rarest genius that ever rose for the ornament and instruction of the human species. Cautious in admitting no principles but such as were founded on experiment, but resolute to adopt every such principle, however new or unusual; from modesty, ignorant of his superiority over the rest of mankind, and thence less careful to accommodate such reasonings to common apprehensions; more anxious to merit than acquire fame:—he was from these causes long unknown to the world; but his reputation at last broke out with a lustre, which scarcely any writer, during his own lifetime, had ever before attained. While Newton seemed to draw off the veil from some of the mysteries of nature, he showed at the same time some of the imperfections of the mechanical philosophy; and thereby restored her ultimate secrets to that obscurity in which they ever did and ever will remain."

The remains of Sir Isaac Newton were interred in Westminster Abbey, where a magnificent monument is erected to his memory, with a Latin inscription, concluding thus:—"Let mortals congratulate themselves that so great an ornament of human nature has existed." His character is shown, by Dr. Brewster, to have been that of the humble and sincere Christian. Of nature, antiquity, and the Holy Scriptures, he was a diligent, sagacious, and faithful interpreter. He maintained by his philosophy the dignity of the Supreme Being, and in his manners he exhibited the simplicity of the Gospel. "I seem to myself," he said, "to be like a child, picking up a shell here and there on the shore of the great ocean of truth." He would hardly admit that he had a genius above other men, but attributed his discoveries to the intentness with which he applied to the study of philosophy. We cannot better close our notice of this great man, than in the words of Pope:

"Nature and nature's laws lay hid in night—
God said, 'let Newton be'—and all was light!"

MAGLIABECCHI.

Antony Magliabecchi was born at Florence, on the 29th of October, in the year 1633. His parents were so poor as to be well satisfied when they got him into the service of a man who sold greens. He had not yet learned to read, but he was perpetually poring over the leaves of old books, that were used as waste paper in his master's shop. A bookseller who lived in the neighborhood, observed this, and knowing that the boy could not read, asked him one day what he meant by staring so much at pieces of printed paper? He said, that he did not know how it was, but that he loved it of all things; that he was very uneasy in the business he was in, and should be the happiest creature in the world if he could live with him, who had always so many books about him.

The bookseller was pleased with this answer; and at last told him, that if his master were willing to part with him, he would take him. Young Magliabecchi was highly delighted, and the more so, when his master, agreeably to the bookseller's desire, gave him leave to go. He went, therefore, directly to his new business. He had not long been there, before he could find out any book that was asked for, as readily as the bookseller himself. In a short period he had learned to read, and then he was always reading when he could find time.

He seems never to have applied himself to any particular study. A love of reading was his ruling passion, and a prodigious memory his great talent. He read all kinds of books, almost indifferently, as they came into his hands, and that with a surprising quickness; yet he retained not only the sense, but often the words and the very manner of spelling.

His extraordinary application and talents soon recommended him to Ermina, librarian to the Cardinal de Medicis, and Marmi, the Grand Duke's librarian. He was by them introduced to the conversation of the learned, and made known at court. He now began to be looked upon everywhere as a prodigy, particularly for his unbounded memory.

In order to make an experiment in respect to this, a gentleman of Florence, who had written a piece, which was to be printed, lent the manuscript to Magliabecchi. Sometime after it had been returned, he came to the librarian with a melancholy face, and told him that by some accident he had lost his manuscript; and seemed almost inconsolable, entreating Magliabecchi, at the same time, to endeavor to recollect as much of it as he possibly could, and write it down. Magliabecchi assured him he would do so, and on setting about it, wrote down the whole, without missing a word.

By treasuring up everything he read, in this wonderful manner, or at least the subject, and all the principal parts of the books he ran over, his head became at last, as one of his acquaintance expressed it, "an universal index, both of titles and matter."

By this time, Magliabecchi was grown so famous for the vast extent of his reading, and his amazing retention of what he had read, that it began to grow common amongst the learned to consult him when they were writing on any subject. Thus, for instance, if a priest was going to compose a panegyric upon any favorite saint, and came to communicate his design to Magliabecchi, he would immediately tell him who had said anything of that saint, and in what part of their works, and that, sometimes, to the number of above a hundred authors. He would tell them not only who had treated of their subject designedly, but of such, also, as had touched upon it incidentally, in writing on other subjects. All this he did with the greatest exactness, naming the author, the book, the words, and often the very number of the page in which the passage referred to was inserted. He did this so often, so readily, and so exactly, that he came at last to be looked upon almost as an oracle, for the ready and full answers that he gave to all questions proposed to him in respect to any subject or science whatever.

It was his great eminence in this way, and his almost inconceivable knowledge of books, that induced the Grand Duke, Cosmo the third, to make him his librarian. What a happiness must it have been to one like Magliabecchi, who delighted in nothing so much as reading, to have the command and use of such a collection of books as that in the Duke's palace! He was also very conversant with the books in the Lorenzo library; and had the keeping of those of Leopoldo, and Francisco Maria, the two cardinals of Tuscany.

Magliabecchi had a local memory, too, of the places where every book stood, in the libraries which he frequented; he seems, indeed, to have carried this even farther. One day the Grand Duke sent for him to ask whether he could get him a book that was particularly scarce. "No, sir," answered Magliabecchi, "for there is but one in the world, and that is in the Grand Signior's library at Constantinople; it is the seventh book on the second shelf, on the right hand, as you go in."

Though Magliabecchi lived so sedentary a life, with such an intense and almost perpetual application to books, yet he arrived to a good old age. He died in his eighty-first year, on the 14th of July, 1714. By his will he left a very fine library, of his own collection, for the use of the public, with a fund to maintain it; and whatever should remain over, to the poor.

In his manner of living, Magliabecchi affected the character of Diogenes; three hard eggs, and a draught or two of water, were his usual repast. When his friends went to see him, they generally found him lolling in a sort of fixed wooden cradle, in the middle of his study, with a multitude of books, some thrown in heaps, and others scattered about the floor, around him. His cradle, or bed, was generally attached to the nearest pile of books by a number of cobwebs: at the entrance of any one, he used to call out, "Don't hurt my spiders!"

JAMES CRICHTON.

JAMES CRICHTON, commonly called 'The Admirable,' son of Robert Crichton, of Eliock, who was Lord Advocate to King James VI., was born in Scotland, in the year 1561. The precise place of his birth is not mentioned, but he received the best part of his education at St. Andrews, at that time the most celebrated seminary in Scotland, where the illustrious Buchanan was one of his masters. At the early age of fourteen, he took his degree of Master of Arts, and was considered a prodigy, not only in abilities, but in actual attainments.

It was the custom of the time for Scotchmen of birth to finish their education abroad, and serve in some foreign army, previously to entering that of their own country. When he was only sixteen or seventeen years old, Crichton's father sent him to the Continent. He had scarcely arrived in Paris, which was then a gay and splendid city, famous for jousting, fencing, and dancing, when he publicly challenged all scholars and philosophers to a disputation at the College of Navarre. He proposed that it should be carried on in any one of twelve specified languages, and have relation to any science or art, whether practical or theoretical. The challenge was accepted; and, as if to show in how little need he stood of preparation, or how lightly he held his adversaries, he spent the six weeks that elapsed between the challenge and the contest, in a continual round of tilting, hunting, and dancing.

On the appointed day, however, and in the contest, he is said to have encountered all the gravest philosophers and divines, and to have acquitted himself to the astonishment of all who heard him. He received the public praises of the president and four of the most eminent professors. The very next day he appeared at a tilting match in the Louvre, and carried off the ring from all his accomplished and experienced competitors.

Enthusiasm was now at its height, particularly among the ladies of the court, and from the versatility of his talents, his youth, the gracefulness of his manners, and the beauty of his person, he was named *L'Admirable*. After serving two years in the army of Henry III., who was engaged in a civil war with his Huguenot subjects, Crichton repaired to Italy, and repeated at Rome, in the presence of the Pope and cardinals, the literary challenge and triumph that had gained him so much honor at Paris.

From Rome he went to Venice, at which gay city he arrived in a depressed state of spirits. None of his Scottish biographers are very willing to acknowledge the fact, but it appears quite certain, that, spite of his noble birth and connexions, he was miserably poor, and became for some time dependent on the bounty of a Venetian printer—the celebrated Aldus Manutius. After a residence of four months at Venice, where his learning, engaging manners, and various accomplishments, excited universal wonder, as is made evident by several Italian writers who were living at the time, and whose lives were published, Crichton went to the neighboring city of Padua, in the learned university of which he reaped fresh honors by Latin poetry, scholastic disputation, an exposition of the errors of Aristotle and his commentators, and as a playful wind-up of the day's labors, a declamation upon the happiness of ignorance.

Another day was fixed for a public disputation in the palace of the bishop of Padua; but this being prevented from taking place, gave some incredulous or envious men the opportunity of asserting that Crichton was a literary impostor, whose acquirements were totally superficial. His reply was a public challenge. The contest, which included the Aristotelian and platonic philosophies, and the mathematics of the time, was prolonged during three days, before an innumerable concourse of people. His friend, Aldus Manutius, who was present at what he calls "this miraculous encounter," says he proved completely victorious, and that he was honored by such a rapture of applause as was never before heard.

Crichton's journeying from university to university to stick up challenges on church doors, and college pillars, though it is said to have been in accordance with customs not then obsolete, certainly attracted some ridicule among the Italians; for Boccalini, after copying one of his placards, in which he announces his arrival, and his readiness to dispute extemporaneously on all subjects, says that a wit wrote under it, "and whosoever wishes to see him, let him go to the Falcon Inn, where he will be shown,"—which is the formula used by showmen for the exhibition of a wild beast, or any other monster.

We next hear of Crichton at Mantua, and as the hero of a combat more tragical than those carried on by the tongue or the pen. A certain Italian gentleman, "of a mighty, able, nimble, and vigorous body, but by nature fierce, cruel, warlike, and audacious, and superlatively expert and dexterous in the use of his weapon," was in the habit of going from one city to another, to challenge men to fight with cold steel, just as Crichton did to challenge them to scholastic combats. This itinerant gladiator, who had marked his way through Italy with blood, had just arrived in Mantua, and killed three young men, the best swordsmen of that city. By universal consent, the Italians were the ablest masters of fence in Europe; a reputation to which they seem still entitled. To encounter a victor among such masters, was a stretch of courage; but Crichton, who had studied the sword from his youth, and who had probably improved himself in the use of the rapier in Italy, did not hesitate to challenge the redoubtable bravo.

Though the duke was unwilling to expose so accomplished a gentleman to so great a hazard, yet, relying upon the report he had heard of his warlike qualifications, he agreed to the proposal; and the time and place being appointed, the whole court attended to behold the performance. At the beginning of the combat, Crichton stood only upon his defence, while the Italian made his attack with such eagerness and fury, that, having exhausted himself, he began to grow weary. The young Scotsman now seized the opportunity of attacking his antagonist in return; which he did with so much dexterity and vigor, that he ran him through the body in three different places, of which wounds he immediately died.

The acclamations of the spectators were loud and long-continued upon this occasion; and it was acknowledged by all, that they had never seen nature second the precepts of art in so lively and graceful a manner as they had beheld it on that day. To crown the glory of the action, Crichton bestowed the rich prize awarded for his victory, upon the widows of the three persons who had lost their lives in fighting with the gladiator.

In consequence of this and his other wonderful performances, the duke of Mantua made choice of him for preceptor to his son, Vicentio de Gonzago, who is represented as being of a riotous temper, and dissolute life. The appointment was highly pleasing to the court. Crichton, to testify his gratitude to his friends and benefactors, and to contribute to their diversion, framed a comedy, wherein he exposed and ridiculed the weaknesses and failures of the several occupations and pursuits in which men are engaged. This composition was regarded as one of the most ingenious satires that ever was made upon mankind. But the most astonishing part of the story, is, that Crichton sustained fifteen characters in the representation of his own play. Among the rest, he acted the divine, the philosopher, the lawyer, the mathematician, the physician, and the soldier, with such inimitable skill, that every time he appeared upon the theatre, he seemed to be a different person.

From being the principal actor in a comedy, Crichton soon became the subject of a dreadful tragedy. One night, during the time of Carnival, as he was walking along the streets of Mantua, and playing upon his guitar, he was attacked by half a dozen people in masks. The assailants found that they had no ordinary person to deal with, for they were not able to maintain their ground against him. At last the leader of the company, being disarmed, pulled off his mask, and begged his life, telling Crichton that he was the prince, his pupil. Crichton immediately fell upon his knees, and expressed his concern for his mistake; alleging that what he had done was only in his own defence, and that if Gonzago had any design upon his life, he might always be master of it. Then, taking his own sword by the point, he presented it to the prince, who immediately received it, and was so irritated by the affront which he thought he had sustained, in being foiled with all his attendants, that he instantly ran Crichton through the heart.

His tragical end excited very great and general lamentation. The whole court of Mantua went three-quarters of a year into mourning for him; and numerous epitaphs and elegies were composed upon his death.

To account in some manner for the extent of Crichton's attainments, it must be recollected that the first scholars of the age were his instructors: for, besides having Rutherford as a tutor, it is stated by Aldus Manutius, that he was also taught by Buchanan, Hessburn, and Robertson; and hence his extraordinary proficiency in the languages, as well as in the sciences, as then taught in the schools of Europe. It must also be recollected that no expense would be spared in his education, as his father was Lord Advocate in Queen Mary's reign, from 1561 to 1573, and his mother, the daughter of Sir James Stuart, was allied to the royal family. It is evident, however, that these advantages were seconded by powers of body and mind rarely united in any human being.

BERONICIUS.

THE history of this man is involved in some obscurity, yet enough is known to show that he was a person of wonderful endowments, and great eccentricity of life and character.

In the year 1674, the celebrated Dutch poet, Antonides Vander Goes, being in Zealand, happened to be in company with a young gentleman, who spoke of the wonderful genius of his language master. Vander Goes expressed a desire to see him, and while they were talking upon the subject, the extraordinary man entered. He was a little, sallow dumpling of a fellow, with fiery eyes, and nimble, fidgety motions; he was withal a sight to see for the raggedness of his garments.

The strange man soon showed that he was drunk, and shortly after took his leave. But in a subsequent interview with the Dutch poet, he fully justified the character his pupil had given him. His great talent lay in being able with almost miraculous quickness, to turn any written theme into Latin or Greek verse. Upon being put to the trial, by Vander Goes, he succeeded, to the admiration of all present.

The poet had just shown him his verses, and asked his opinion of them. Beronicius read them twice, praised them, and said, "What should hinder me from turning them into Latin instantly?" The company viewed him with curiosity, and encouraged him by saying, "Well, pray let us see what you can do." In the meantime, the man appeared to be startled. He trembled from head to foot, as if possessed. However, he selected an epigram from the poems, and asked the precise meaning of two or three Dutch words, of which he did not clearly understand the force, and requested that he might be allowed to Latinize the name of *Hare*, which occurred in the poem, in some manner so as not to lose the pun. They agreed; and he immediately said, "I have already found it,—I shall call him *Dasypus*," which signifies an animal with rough legs, and is likewise taken by the Greeks for a hare. "Now, read a couple of lines at a time to me, and I shall give them in Latin," said he;—upon which a poet named Buizero, began to read to him, and Beronicius burst out in the following verses:—

> Egregia Dasypus referens virtute leonem
> In bello, adversus Britonas super æquora gesto,
> Impavidus pelago stetit, aggrediente molossum.
> Agmine quem tandem glans ferrea misit ad astra,
> Vindictæ cupidum violato jure profundi.
> Advena, quisquis ades, Zelandæ encomia gentis
> Ista refer, lepores demta quod pelle leonem,
> Assumant, quotquot nostro versantur in orbe.
> Epitaphium Herois Adriani de Haze, ex Belgico versum.

When the poet had finished, he laughed till his sides shook; at the same time he was jeering and pointing at the company, who appeared surprised at his having, contrary to their expectations, acquitted himself so well; everybody highly praised him, which elated him so much that he scratched his head three or four times; and fixing his fiery eyes on the ground, repeated without hesitation, the same epigram in Greek verse, calling out, "There ye have it in Greek." Every one was astonished, which set him a-laughing and jeering for a quarter of an hour.

The Greek he repeated so rapidly, that no one could write from his recitation. John Frederick Gymnick, professor of the Greek language at Duisburgh, who was one of the auditors, said that he esteemed the Greek version as superior to the Latin. Beronicius was afterwards examined in various ways, and gave such proofs of his wonderful learning, as amazed all the audience.

This singular genius spoke several languages so perfectly, that each might have passed for his mother tongue; especially Italian, French, and English. But Greek was his favorite, and he used it as correctly and as fluently as if he had always spoken it. He knew by heart the whole of Horace and Virgil, the greatest part of Cicero, and both the Plinys; and would immediately, if a line were mentioned, repeat the whole passage, and tell the exact work, volume, chapter, and verse, of all these, and many more, especially poets. The works of Juvenal were so interwoven with his brain, that he retained every word.

Of the Greek poets, he had Homer strongly imprinted on his memory, together with some of the comedies of Aristophanes; he could directly turn to any line required, and repeat the whole contiguous passage. His Latin was full of words selected from the most celebrated writers.

The reader will probably be desirous of knowing to what country Beronicius belonged; but this is a secret he never would disclose. When he was asked what was his native land, he always answered, "that the country of every one, was that in which he could live most comfortably." It was well known that he had wandered about many years in France, England, and the Netherlands, carrying his whole property with him. He was sometimes told that he deserved to be a professor in a college;—but his reply was, that he could have no pleasure in such a worm-like life.

Strange to say, this eccentric being gained his living chiefly by sweeping chimneys, grinding knives and scissors, and other mean occupations. But his chief delight was in pursuing the profession of a juggler, mountebank, or merry-andrew, among the lowest rabble. He never gave himself any concern about his food or raiment; for it was equal to him whether he was dressed like a nobleman or a beggar. His hours of relaxation from his studies were chiefly spent in paltry wine-houses, with the meanest company, where he would sometimes remain a whole week, or more, drinking without rest or intermission.

His miserable death afforded reason to believe that he perished whilst intoxicated, for he was found dead at Middleburgh, drowned and smothered in mud, which circumstance is alluded to in the epitaph which the before named poet, Buizero, wrote upon him, and which was as follows:—

> Here lies a wonderful genius,
> He lived and died like a beast;
> He was a most uncommon satyr—
> He lived in wine, and died in water.

This is all that is known of Beronicius. The poet, Vander Goes, often witnessed the display of his talents, and he says that he could at once render the newspapers into Greek and Latin verse. Professor John de Raay, who was living at the time of Beronicius's death, which occurred in 1676, saw and affirms the same wonderful fact.

MASTER CLENCH.

OF this astonishing youth, we have no information except what is furnished by the following account, extracted from Mr. Evelyn's diary, of 1689, very shortly after the landing of William III. in England.

"I dined," says Mr. Evelyn, "at the Admiralty, where a child of twelve years old was brought in, the son of Dr. Clench, of the most prodigious maturity of knowledge, for I cannot call it altogether memory, but something more extraordinary. Mr. Pepys and myself examined him, not in any method, but with promiscuous questions, which required judgment and discernment, to answer so readily and pertinently.

"There was not anything in chronology, history, geography, the several systems of astronomy, courses of the stars, longitude, latitude, doctrine of the spheres, courses and sources of rivers, creeks, harbors, eminent cities, boundaries of countries, not only in Europe, but in every part of the earth, which he did not readily resolve, and demonstrate his knowledge of, readily drawing with a pen anything he would describe.

"He was able not only to repeat the most famous things which are left us in any of the Greek or Roman histories, monarchies, republics, wars, colonies, exploits by sea and land, but all the Sacred Scriptures of the Old and New Testaments; the succession of all the monarchies, Babylonian, Persian, Greek and Roman; with all the lower emperors, popes, heresiarchs, and councils; what they were called about; what they determined; or in the controversy about Easter; the tenets of the Sabellians, Arians, Nestorians; and the difference between St. Cyprian and Stephen about re-baptization; the schisms.

"We leaped from that to other things totally different,—to Olympic years and synchronisms; we asked him questions which could not be answered without considerable meditation and judgment; nay, of some particulars of the civil wars; of the digest and code. He gave a stupendous account of both natural and moral philosophy, and even of metaphysics.

"Having thus exhausted ourselves, rather than this wonderful child, or angel rather, for he was as beautiful and lovely in countenance as in knowledge, we concluded with asking him, if, in all he had ever heard or read of, he had ever met with anything which was like the expedition of the Prince of Orange, with so small a force, as to obtain three kingdoms without any contest. After a little thought, he told us that he knew of nothing that resembled it, so much as the coming of Constantine the Great out of Great Britain, through France and Italy, so tedious a march, to meet Maxentius, whom he overthrew at Pons Melvius, with very little conflict, and at the very gates of Rome, which he entered, and was received with triumph, and obtained the empire not of three kingdoms only, but of the then known world.

"He was perfect in the Latin authors, spoke French naturally, and gave us a description of France, Italy, Savoy and Spain, anciently and modernly divided; as also of ancient Greece, Scythia, and the northern countries and tracts.

"He answered our questions without any set or formal repetitions, as one who had learned things without book, but as if he minded other things, going about the room, and toying with a parrot, seeming to be full of play, of a lively, sprightly temper, always smiling, and exceedingly pleasant; without the least levity, rudeness, or childishness."

THIS extraordinary man was born in 1705, at Elmeton, in Derbyshire. His father was a schoolmaster; and yet, from some strange neglect, Jedediah was never taught either to read or write. So great, however, were his natural talents for calculation, that he became remarkable for his knowledge of the relative proportions of numbers, their powers and progressive denominations. To these objects he applied all the powers of his mind, and his attention was so constantly rivetted upon them, that he was often totally abstracted from external objects. Even when he did notice them, it was only with respect to their numbers. If any space of time happened to be mentioned before him, he would presently inform the company that it contained so many minutes; and if any distance, he would assign the number of hair-breadths in it, even though no question were asked him.

Being, on one occasion, required to multiply 456 by 378, he gave the product by mental arithmetic, as soon as a person in company had completed it in the common way. Being requested to work it audibly, that his method might be known, he first multiplied 456 by 5, which produced 2,280; this he again multiplied by 20, and found the product 45,600, which was the multiplicand, multiplied by 100. This product he again multiplied by 3, which gave 136,800, the product of the multiplicand by 300. It remained, therefore, to multiply this by 78, which he effected by multiplying 2,280, or the product of the multiplicand, multiplied by 5, by 15, as 5 times 15 is 75. This product being 34,200, he added to 136,800, which gave 171,000, being the amount of 375 times 456. To complete his operation, therefore, he multiplied 456 by 3, which produced 1,368, and this being added to 171,000, yielded 172,368, as the product of 456 multiplied by 378.

From these particulars, it appears that Jedediah's method of calculation was entirely his own, and that he was so little acquainted with the common rules of arithmetic, as to multiply first by 5, and the product by 20, to find the amount when multiplied by 100, which the addition of two ciphers to the multiplicand would have given at once.

A person who had heard of these efforts of memory, once meeting with him accidentally, proposed the following question, in order to try his calculating powers. If a field be 423 yards long, and 383 broad, what is the area? After the figures were read to him distinctly, he gave the true product, 162,009 yards, in the space of two minutes; for the proposer observed by the watch, how long it took him. The same person asked how many acres the said field measured; and in eleven minutes, he replied, 33 acres, 1 rood, 35 perches, 20 yards and a quarter. He was then asked how many barley-corns would reach eight miles. In a minute and a half, he answered 1,520,640. The next question was: supposing the distance between London and York to be 204 miles, how many times will a coach-wheel turn round in that space, allowing the circumference of that wheel to be six yards. In thirteen minutes, he answered, 59,840 times.

On another occasion a person proposed to him this question: in a body, the three sides of which are 23,145,789 yards, 5,642,732 yards, and 54,965 yards, how many cubic eighths of an inch? In about five hours Jedediah had accurately solved this intricate problem, though in the midst of business, and surrounded by more than a hundred laborers.

Next to figures, the only objects of Jedediah's curiosity were the king and royal family. So strong was his desire to see them, that in the beginning of the spring of 1754, he walked up to London for that purpose, but returned disappointed, as his majesty had removed to Kensington just as he arrived in town. He was, however, introduced to the Royal Society, whom he called the *Folk of the Siety Court.* The gentlemen present asked him several questions in arithmetic to try his abilities, and dismissed him with a handsome present.

During his residence in the metropolis, he was taken to see the tragedy of King Richard the Third, performed at Drury Lane, Garrick being one of the actors. It was expected that the novelty of everything in that place, together with the splendor of the surrounding objects, would have filled him with astonishment; or that his passions would have been roused in some degree, by the action of the performers, even though he might not fully comprehend the dialogue. This, certainly, was a rational idea; but his thoughts were far otherwise employed. During the dances, his attention was engaged in reckoning the number of steps; after a fine piece of music, he declared that the innumerable sounds produced by the instruments perplexed him beyond measure, but he counted the words uttered by Mr. Garrick, in the whole course of the entertainment; and declared that in this part of the business, he had perfectly succeeded.

Heir to no fortune, and educated to no particular profession, Jedediah Buxton supported himself by the labor of his hands. His talents, had they been properly cultivated, might have qualified him for acting a distinguished part on the theatre of life; he, nevertheless, pursued the "noiseless tenor of his way," content if he could satisfy the wants of nature, and procure a daily subsistence for himself and family. He was married and had several children. He died in the year 1775, aged seventy years. Though a man of wonderful powers of arithmetical calculation, and generally regarded as a prodigy in his way—it is still obvious that, after the practice of years, he was incapable of solving questions, which Zerah Colburn, at the age of six or seven years, answered in the space of a few seconds.

WILLIAM GIBSON.

WILLIAM GIBSON was born in the year 1720, at the village of Bolton, in Westmoreland, England. On the death of his father, he put himself to a farmer to learn his business. When he was about eighteen or nineteen, he rented a small farm of his own, at a place called Hollins, where he applied himself assiduously to study.

A short time previous to this, he had admired the operation of figures, but labored under every disadvantage, for want of education. As he had not yet been taught to read, he got a few lessons in English, and was soon enabled to comprehend a plain author. He then purchased a treatise on arithmetic; and though he could not write, he soon became so expert a calculator, from mental operations only, that he could tell, without setting down a figure, the product of any two numbers multiplied together, although the multiplier and the multiplicand each of them consisted of nine figures. It was equally astonishing that he could answer, in the same manner, questions in division, in decimal fractions, or in the extraction of the square or cube roots, where such a multiplicity of figures is often required in the operation. Yet at this time he did not know that any merit was due to himself, conceiving that the capacity of other people was like his own.

Finding himself still laboring under farther difficulties for want of a knowledge of writing, he taught himself to write a tolerable hand. As he had not heard of mathematics, he had no idea of anything, in regard to numbers, beyond what he had learned. He thought himself a master of figures, and challenged all his companions and the members of a society he attended, to a trial. Something, however, was proposed to him concerning Euclid. As he did not understand the meaning of the word, he was silent; but afterwards found it meant a book, containing the elements of geometry; this he purchased, and applied himself very diligently to the study of it, and against the next meeting he was prepared with an answer in this new science.

He now found himself launching out into a field, of which before he had no conception. He continued his geometrical studies; and as the demonstration of the different propositions in Euclid depend entirely upon a recollection of some of those preceding, his memory was of the utmost service to him. Besides, it was a study exactly adapted to his mind; and while he was attending to the business of his farm, and humming over some tune or other, his attention was often engaged with some of his geometrical propositions. A few figures with a piece of chalk, upon the knee of his breeches, or any other convenient spot, were all he needed to clear up the most difficult parts of the science.

He now began to be struck with the works of nature, and paid particular attention to the theory of the earth, the moon, and the rest of the planets belonging to this system, of which the sun is the centre; and considering the distance and magnitude of the different bodies belonging to it, and the distance of the fixed stars, he soon conceived each of them to be the centre of a different system. He well considered the law of gravity, and that of the centripetal and centrifugal forces, and the cause of the ebbing and flowing of the tides; also the projection of the sphere—stereographic, orthographic, and gnomical; also trigonometry and astronomy. By this time he was possessed of a small library.

He next turned his thoughts to algebra, and took up Emerson's treatise on that subject, and went through it with great success. He also grounded himself in the art of navigation and the principles of mechanics; likewise the doctrine of motion, of falling bodies, and the elements of optics, &c., as a preliminary to fluxions, which had but lately been discovered by Sir Isaac Newton; as the boundary of the mathematics, he went through conic sections, &c. Though he experienced some difficulty at his first entrance, yet he did not rest till he made himself master of both a fluxion and a flowing quantity. As he had paid a similar attention to the intermediate parts, he soon became so conversant with every branch of the mathematics, that no question was ever proposed to him which he could not answer.

He used to take pleasure in solving the arithmetical questions then common in the magazines, but his answers were seldom inserted, except by or in the name of some other person, for he had no ambition to make his abilities known. He frequently had questions from his pupils and other gentlemen in London; from the universities of Oxford and Cambridge, and different parts of the country, as well as from the university of Gottingen in Germany. These, however difficult, he never failed to answer; and from the minute inquiry he made into natural philosophy, there was scarcely a phenomenon in nature, that ever came to his knowledge or observation, but he could, in some measure at least, reasonably account for it.

He went by the name of Willy-o'-th'-Hollins, for many years after he left his residence in that place. The latter portion of his life was spent in the neighborhood of Cartmell, where he was best known by the name of Willy Gibson, still continuing his former occupation. For the last forty years he kept a school of about eight or ten gentlemen, who boarded and lodged at his own farm-house; and having a happy turn in explaining his ideas, he formed a great number of very able mathematicians, as well as expert accountants. This self-taught philosopher and wonderful man, died on the 4th of October, 1792, at Blaith, near Cartmell, in consequence of a fall, leaving behind him a widow and ten children.

EDMUND STONE.

Of the life of this extraordinary man we have little information. He was probably born in Argyleshire, Scotland, at the close of the seventeenth century. His father was gardener to the Duke of Argyle, and the son assisted him. The duke was walking one day in his garden, when he observed a Latin copy of Newton's Principia, lying on the grass, and supposing it had been brought from his own library, called some one to carry it back to its place. Upon this, young Stone, who was in his eighteenth year, claimed the book as his own. "Yours!" replied the duke; "do you understand geometry, Latin, and Newton?" "I know a little of them," said the young man.

The duke was surprised, and having a taste for the sciences, he entered into conversation with the young mathematician. He proposed several inquiries, and was astonished at the force, the accuracy and the clearness of his answers. "But how," said the duke, "came you by the knowledge of all these things?" Stone replied, "A servant taught me to read ten years since. Does one need to know anything more than the twenty-six letters, in order to learn everything else that one wishes?"

The duke's curiosity was now greatly increased, and he sat down upon a bank and requested a detail of the whole process by which he had acquired such knowledge. "I first learned to read," said Stone; "afterwards, when the masons were at work at your house, I approached them one day, and observed that the architect used a rule and compass, and that he made calculations. I inquired what might be the meaning and use of these things; and I was informed that there was a science called arithmetic. I purchased a book of arithmetic, and studied it. I was told that there was another science, called geometry. I bought the necessary books, and learned geometry.

"By reading, I found there were good books on these two sciences in Latin; I therefore bought a dictionary and learned Latin. I understood, also, that there were good books of the same kind in French; I bought a dictionary and learned French; and this, my lord, is what I have done. It seems to me that we may learn everything when we know the twenty-six letters of the alphabet."

Under the duke's patronage, Stone rose to be a very considerable mathematician, and was elected a member of the Royal Society of London, in 1725. He seems to have lost the favor of the Duke of Argyle, for, in the latter part of his life, he gave lessons in mathematics, and at last died in poverty.

RICHARD EVELYN.

JOHN EVELYN, a very learned English writer, was born in 1620, and died in 1706. He published several works, all of which are valuable. His treatises upon Natural History are greatly valued. He kept a diary, which has been published, and which contains much that is interesting. Of one of his children, who died early, he gives us the following account:

"After six fits of ague, died, in the year 1658, my son Richard, five years and three days old, but, at that tender age, a prodigy of wit and understanding; for beauty of body, a very angel; for endowment of mind, of incredible and rare hopes. To give only a little taste of some of them, and thereby glory to God:

"At two years and a half old, he could perfectly read any of the English, Latin, French, or Gothic letters, pronouncing the three first languages exactly. He had, before the fifth year, not only skill to read most written hands, but to decline all the nouns, conjugate the verbs regular and most of the irregular; learned Pericles through; got by heart almost the entire vocabulary of Latin and French primitives and words, could make congruous syntax, turn English into Latin, and *vice versa*, construe and prove what he read, and did the government and use of relative verbs, substantives, ellipses, and many figures and tropes, and made a considerable progress in Comenius's Janua; began himself to write legibly, and had a strong passion for Greek.

"The number of verses he could recite was enormous; and when seeing a Plautus in one's hand, he asked what book it was, and being told it was comedy and too difficult for him, he wept for sorrow. Strange was his apt and ingenious application of fables and morals, for he had read Æsop. He had a wonderful disposition to mathematics, having by heart divers propositions of Euclid, that were read to him in play, and he would make lines and demonstrate them.

"As to his piety, astonishing were his applications of Scripture upon occasion, and his sense of God: he had learned all his catechism early, and understood the historical part of the Bible and Testament to a wonder—how Christ came to mankind; and how, comprehending these necessaries himself, his godfathers were discharged of their promise. These and like illuminations, far exceeding his age and experience, considering the prettiness of his address and behavior cannot but leave impressions in me at the memory of him. When one told him how many days a Quaker had fasted, he replied, that was no wonder, for Christ had said 'man should not live by bread alone, but by the word of God.'

"He would, of himself, select the most pathetic Psalms, and chapters out of Job, to read to his maid during his sickness, telling her, when she pitied him, that all God's children must suffer affliction. He declaimed against the vanities of the world, before he had seen any. Often he would desire those who came to see him, to pray by him, and a year before he fell sick, to kneel and pray with him, alone in some corner. How thankfully would he receive admonition! how soon be reconciled! how indifferent, yet continually cheerful! He would give grave advice to his brother John, bear with his impertinences, and say he was but a child.

"If he heard of, or saw any new thing, he was unquiet till he was told how it was made; he brought to us all such difficulties as he found in books, to be expounded. He had learned by heart divers sentences in Greek and Latin, which on occasions he would produce even to wonder. He was all life, all prettiness, far from morose, sullen, or childish in anything he said or did. The last time he had been at church, which was at Greenwich, I asked him, according to custom, what he remembered of the sermon. 'Two good things, father,' said he, '*bonum gratiæ*, and *bonum gloriæ*;" the excellence of grace, and the excellence of glory,—with a just account of what the preacher said.

"The day before he died, he called to me, and, in a more serious manner than usual, told me, that for all I loved him so dearly, I should give my house, land, and all my fine things to his brother Jack,—he should have none of them; and next morning, when he found himself ill, and I persuaded him to keep his hands in bed, he demanded whether he might pray to God with his hands unjoined; and a little after, whilst in great agony, whether he should not offend God by using his holy name so often by calling for ease.

"What shall I say of his frequent pathetical ejaculations uttered of himself: 'Sweet Jesus, save me, deliver me, pardon my sins, let thine angels receive me!' So early knowledge, so much piety and perfection! But thus God, having dressed up a saint fit for himself, would no longer permit him with us, unworthy of the future fruits of this incomparable, hopeful blossom. Such a child I never saw! for such a child I bless God, in whose bosom he is! May I and mine become as this little child, which now follows the child Jesus, that lamb of God, in a white robe, whithersoever he goes! Even so, Lord Jesus, let thy will be done. Thou gavest him to us, thou hast taken him from us; blessed be the name of the Lord! That I had anything acceptable to thee was from thy grace alone, since from me he had nothing but sin; but that thou hast pardoned, blessed be my God forever! Amen."

QUENTIN MATSYS.

THIS great painter was born at Antwerp, in 1460, and followed the trade of a blacksmith and farrier, till he approached manhood. His health at that time was feeble, and rendered him unfit for so laborious a pursuit; he therefore undertook to execute lighter work. He constructed an iron railing around a well near the great church of Antwerp, which was greatly admired for its delicacy and the devices with which it was ornamented. He also executed an iron balustrade for the college of Louvain, which displayed extraordinary taste and skill.

His father had died, when he was young, leaving him and his mother entirely destitute. Notwithstanding his feeble constitution, he was obliged to support both himself and her. While necessity thus urged him, his taste guided his efforts toward works of art. At Louvain there was an annual procession of lepers, who were accustomed to distribute little images of saints upon that occasion. Matsys devoted himself to the making of these, in which he was very successful.

MATSYS' WELL, AT ANTWERP.

He had now reached the age of twenty, when it appears that he fell in love with the daughter of a painter, of some cleverness, in Antwerp. His affection was returned, but when he applied to the father to obtain his consent to their union, he was answered by a flat refusal, and the declaration, that no man but a painter, as good as himself, should wed his daughter. Matsys endeavored in vain to overcome this resolution, and finally, despairing of other means to accomplish the object which now engrossed his whole soul, he determined to become a painter. The difficulties in his way vanished before that confidence which genius inspires, and taking advantage of his leisure hours, he began to instruct himself secretly in the art of painting. His progress was rapid, and the time of his triumph speedily approached.

He was one day on a visit to his mistress, where he found a picture on the easel of her father, and nearly finished. The old man was absent, and Quentin, seizing the pencil, painted a bee upon a flower in the foreground of the painting, and departed. The artist soon returned, and in sitting down to his picture, immediately discovered the insect, which had so strangely intruded itself upon his canvass. It was so life-like as to make it seem a real insect, that had been deceived by the mimic flower, and had just alighted upon it. The artist was in raptures, for it appears that he had a heart to appreciate excellence, even if it was not his own. He inquired of his daughter who had painted the bee. Though the details of the interview which followed are not handed down to us, we may be permitted to fill up the scene.

Father. Tell me, child, who painted the insect?

Daughter. Who painted the insect? Really, how should I know?

F. You ought to know,—you must know. It was not one of my pupils. It is beyond them all.

D. Is it as good as you could have done yourself, father?

F. Yes; I never painted anything better in my life. It is like nature's own work, it is so light, so true; on my soul, I was deceived at first, and was about to brush the insect away with my handkerchief.

D. And so, father, you think it is as well as you could have done yourself?

F. Yes.

D. Well, I will send for Quentin Matsys; perhaps he can tell you who did it.

F. Aye, girl, is that it? Did Quentin do it? Then he is a clever fellow, and shall marry you.

Whether such a dialogue as this actually took place, we cannot say; but it appears that Quentin's acknowledged excellence as an artist soon won the painter's consent, and he married the daughter. From this time he devoted his life to the art which love alone had at first induced him to pursue. He soon rose to the highest rank in his profession, and has left behind him an enduring fame. Though he was destitute of early education, and never had the advantage of studying the great masters of the Italian school, he rivalled, in some respects, even their best productions. His designs were correct and true to nature, and his coloring was forcible. His pictures are now scarce and command great prices. One of them, called the Two Misers, is in the Royal Gallery of Windsor, England, and is greatly admired. Matsys died at Antwerp, in 1529.

WEST.

Benjamin West was born at Springfield, Pennsylvania, October 10, 1738. His father was a merchant, and Benjamin was the tenth child. The first six years of his life passed away in calm uniformity, leaving only the placid remembrance of enjoyment. In the month of June, 1745, one of his sisters who was married, came with her infant daughter to spend a few days at her father's. When the child was asleep in her cradle, Mrs. West invited her daughter to gather flowers in the garden, and committed the infant to the care of Benjamin, during their absence; giving him a fan to drive away the flies from molesting his little charge.

After some time, the child happened to smile in its sleep, and its beauty attracted the boy's attention. He looked at it with a pleasure, which he never before experienced; and observing some paper on a table, together with pens, and red and black ink, he seized them with agitation, and endeavored to delineate a portrait, although at this period, he was only in the seventh year of his age.

Hearing the approach of his mother and sister, he endeavored to conceal what he had been doing; but the old lady observing his confusion, inquired what he was about, and requested him to show her the paper. He obeyed, entreating her not to be angry. Mrs. West, after looking at the drawing with evident pleasure, said to her daughter, "I declare, he has made a likeness of little Sally;" she kissed him with much fondness and satisfaction. This encouraged him to say that if it would give her any pleasure, he would make pictures of the flowers which she held in her hand; for the instinct of his genius was now awakened, and he felt that he could imitate the forms of those things which pleased his sight.

Christ healing the sick.

Some time after this, Benjamin having heard that pencils for painting were made in Europe of camel's hair, determined to manufacture a substitute, for his own use: accordingly, seizing upon a black cat, kept in the family, he extracted the requisite hairs from her tail for his first brush, and afterwards pillaged it again for others.

Such was the commencement of a series of efforts which raised West to be a favorite painter in England, and, at last, president of the Royal Academy of London. His parents were Quakers, but they encouraged his efforts. He, however, had no advantages, and for some time he was obliged to pursue his labors with such pencils as he made himself, and with red and yellow colors, which he learned to prepare from some Indians who roamed about the town of Springfield: to these, his mother added a little indigo.

He had a cousin by the name of Pennington, who was a merchant, and having seen some of his sketches, sent him a box of paints and pencils, with canvass prepared, and six engravings. The possession of this treasure almost prevented West's sleeping. He now went into a garret as soon as it was light, and began his work. He was so wrapt up in his task, as to stay from school.

This he continued till his master called to inquire what had become of him. A search was consequently made, and he was found at his easel, in the garret. His mother's anger soon subsided, when she saw his picture, now nearly finished. He had not servilely copied one of the engravings, as might have been expected, but had formed a new picture by combining the parts of several of them. His mother kissed the boy with rapture, and procured the pardon of his father and teacher. Mr. Galt, who wrote West's life, says, that, sixty-seven years after, he had the pleasure of seeing this very piece, hanging by the side of the sublime picture of Christ Rejected.

Young West's fame was soon spread abroad, and he was shortly crowded with applications for portraits, of which he painted a considerable number. He was now of an age to require a decision of his parents in respect to the profession he was to follow, in life. They deliberated long and anxiously upon this subject, and at last concluded to refer the matter to the society of Quakers to which they belonged. These decided, that, although they did not acknowledge the utility of painting to mankind, yet they would allow the youth to follow a path for which he had so evident a genius.

At the age of eighteen, he established himself in Philadelphia, as a portrait painter, and afterwards spent some time at New York, in the same capacity. In both places, his success was considerable. In 1760, aided by friends, he proceeded to Italy, to study his art; in 1763, he went to London, where he soon became established for life. The king, George III., was his steadfast friend, and he became painter to his majesty. He was offered a salary of seven hundred pounds a year, by the Marquis of Rockingham, to embellish his mansion at Yorkshire with historical paintings, but this he declined.

On the death of Sir Joshua Reynolds, he was elected president of the Royal Academy, and took his place in March, 1792. In his sixty-fifth year, he painted his great picture of Christ healing the sick, to aid the Quakers of Philadelphia in the erection of a hospital for that city. It was so much admired that he was offered no less than fifteen thousand dollars for this performance. He accepted the offer, as he was not rich, upon condition that he should be allowed to make a copy for the Friends of Philadelphia, for whom he had intended it. This great picture, of which we give an engraving, was long exhibited at Philadelphia, and the profits essentially aided the benevolent object which suggested the picture.

West continued to pursue his profession, and painted several pictures of great size, under the idea that his talent was best suited to such performances. In 1817, his wife, with whom he had long lived in uninterrupted happiness, died, and he followed her in 1820. If his standing, as an artist, is not of the highest rank, it is still respectable, and his history affords a striking instance of a natural fitness and predilection for a particular pursuit. If we consider the total want of encouragement to painting, in a Quaker family, in a country town in Pennsylvania, more than a century ago, and advert to the spontaneous display of his taste and its persevering cultivation, we shall see that nature seems to have given him an irresistible impulse in the direction of the art to which he devoted his life.

West was tall, firmly built, and of a fair complexion. He always preserved something of the sedate, even and sober manners of the sect to which his parents belonged; in disposition, he was mild, liberal and generous. He seriously impaired his fortune by the aid he rendered to indigent young artists. His works were very numerous, and the exhibition and sale of those in his hands, at the time of his death, yielded a handsome sum to his family. Though his early education was neglected, he supplied the defect by study and observation, and his writings connected with the arts are very creditable to him as a man, a philosopher and an artist.

BERRETINI.

PIETRO BERRETINI was born 1596, at Cortona, in Italy. He is called Pietro Da Cortona, from the place of his birth. Even when a child, he evinced uncommon genius for painting; but he appeared likely to remain in obscurity and ignorance, as the extreme poverty of his situation precluded him from the usual means of improving natural talent. He struggled, however, with his difficulties, and ultimately overcame every obstacle which opposed him.

When twelve years old, he went, alone and on foot, to Florence, the seat of the fine arts, possessed of no money, and, in fact, completely without resources of any kind. Notwithstanding this gloomy aspect of affairs, he did not lose his courage, but still persevered in a resolution he had thus early formed, to become "an eminent painter." Pietro knew of no person to whom he could apply for assistance in Florence, excepting a poor boy from Cortona, who was then a scullion in the kitchen of Cardinal Sachetti. Pietro sought him out; his little countryman welcomed him very kindly, shared with him his humble meal, offered him the half of his little bed as a lodging, and promised to supply him with food from the spare meat of his kitchen.

Thus provided with the necessaries of life, Pietro applied himself with indefatigable diligence to the art to which he had devoted himself, and soon made such progress in it, as, in his own opinion, amply recompensed him for all the toil, privation and difficulties he had undergone. It was interesting to observe this poor, destitute child, without a friend to guide his conduct or direct his studies, devoting himself with such unceasing assiduity to his own improvement. His little friend, the scullion, did not relax in kindness and generosity towards him; for all that he possessed he shared with Pietro, and the latter, in return, brought him all the drawings he made, and with these he adorned the walls of the little garret in which they slept.

Pietro was in the habit of wandering to a distance from Florence, to take views of the beautiful scenery in the environs of that city. When night overtook him unawares, which was often the case, he very contentedly slept under the shelter of a tree, and arose as soon as daylight dawned to renew his employment. During his absence, on one of these excursions, some of his pictures accidentally fell into the hands of Cardinal Sachetti, who, struck with the merit that distinguished them, inquired by what artist they were executed. He was not a little astonished to hear that they were the performances of a poor child, who had, for more than two years, been supported by the bounty of one of his kitchen boys. The cardinal desired to see Pietro; and when the young artist was brought before him, he received him in a kind manner, assigned him a pension and placed him as a scholar under one of the best painters of Rome.

Pietro afterwards became a very eminent painter, and made the most grateful returns to his friend, the scullion, for the kindness he had shown him in poverty and wretchedness. He spent the latter part of his life at Rome, where he enjoyed the patronage of successive pontiffs, and was made a knight by Pope Alexander III. He was an architect as well as a painter, and designed the church of Saint Martin, at Rome, where he was buried, and to which he bequeathed a hundred thousand crowns. He died 1669, full of wealth and honors. His works display admirable talents, and his history affords a striking example of native genius, overcoming all obstacles, and hewing its way to success in that pursuit for which nature had seemed to create it.

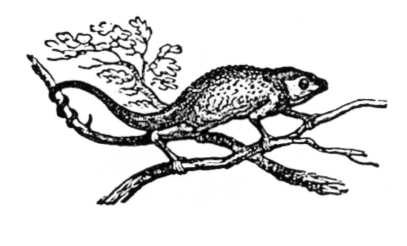

HENRY KIRK WHITE.

THIS youthful bard, whose premature death was so sincerely regretted by every admirer of genius, was the son of a butcher of Nottingham, England, and born March 21, 1788. He manifested an ardent love of reading in his infancy; this was, indeed, a passion to which everything else gave way. "I could fancy," says his eldest sister, "that I see him in his little chair, with a large book upon his knee, and my mother calling, 'Henry, my love, come to dinner,' which was repeated so often without being regarded, that she was obliged to change the tone of her voice, before she could rouse him."

When he was seven years old, he would creep unperceived into the kitchen, to teach the servant to read and write; and he continued this for some time before it was discovered that he had been thus laudably employed. He wrote a tale of a Swiss emigrant, which was probably his first composition, and gave it to this servant, being ashamed to show it to his mother. "The consciousness of genius," says his biographer, Mr. Southey, "is always, at first, accompanied by this diffidence; it is a sacred, solitary feeling. No forward child, however extraordinary the promise of his childhood, ever produced anything truly great."

When Henry was about eleven years old, he one day wrote a separate theme for every boy in his class, which consisted of about twelve or fourteen. The master said he had never known them write so well upon any subject before, and could not refrain from expressing his astonishment at the excellence of Henry's own composition.

At the age of thirteen, he wrote a poem, "On being confined to school one pleasant morning in spring," from which the following is an extract:

> "How gladly would my soul forego
> All that arithmeticians know,
> Or stiff grammarians quaintly teach,
> Or all that industry can reach,
> To taste each morn of all the joys
> That with the laughing sun arise;
> And unconstrained to rove along
> The bushy brakes and glens among;
> And woo the muse's gentle power
> In unfrequented rural bower;
> But ah! such heaven-approaching joys
> Will never greet my longing eyes;
> Still will they cheat in vision fine,
> Yet never but in fancy shine."

The parents of Henry were anxious to put him to some trade, and when he was nearly fourteen, he was placed at a stocking loom, with the view, at some future period, of getting a situation in a hosier's warehouse; but the youth did not conceive that nature had intended to doom him to spend seven years of his life in folding up stockings, and he remonstrated with his friends against the employment. His temper and tone of mind at this period, are displayed in the following extracts from his poems:

————————"Men may rave,
And blame and censure me, that I don't tie
My ev'ry thought down to the desk, and spend
The morning of my life in adding figures
With accurate monotony; that so
The good things of this world may be my lot,
And I might taste the blessedness of wealth.
But oh! I was not made for money-getting."

*   *   *   *   *   *   *

————————"For as still
I tried to cast, with school dexterity,
The interesting sums, my vagrant thoughts
Would quick revert to many a woodland haunt,
Which fond remembrance cherished; and the pen
Dropt from my senseless fingers, as I pictur'd
In my mind's eye, how on the shores of Trent
I erewhile wander'd with my early friends
In social intercourse."

*   *   *   *   *   *   *

"Yet still, oh contemplation! I do love
T' indulge thy solemn musings; still the same
With thee alone I know how to melt and weep,
In thee alone delighting. Why along
The dusty track of commerce should I toil,
When with an easy competence content,
I can alone be happy, where with thee
I may enjoy the loveliness of nature,
And loose the wings of Fancy? Thus alone
Can I partake of happiness on earth;
And to be happy here is man's chief end,
For, to be happy, he must needs be good."

Young White was soon removed from the loom to the office of a solicitor, which afforded a less obnoxious employment. He became a member of a literary society in Nottingham, and delivered an extempore lecture on genius, in which he displayed so much talent, that he received the unanimous thanks of the society, and they elected him their professor of literature.

At the age of fifteen, he gained a silver medal for a translation from Horace; and the following year, a pair of globes, for an imaginary tour from London to Edinburgh. He determined upon trying for this prize one evening when at tea with his family, and at supper, he read them his performance. In his seventeenth year, he published a small volume of poems which possessed considerable merit.

Soon after, he was sent to Cambridge, and entered Saint John's College, where he made the most rapid progress. But the intensity of his studies ruined his constitution, and he fell a victim to his ardent thirst for knowledge. He died October 19, 1806, leaving behind him several poems and letters, which gave earnest of the high rank he would have attained in the republic of letters, had his life been spared. His productions were published, with an interesting memoir, by Mr. Southey.

MOZART.

John Chrysostomus Wolfgang Amadeus Mozart, was born at Salzburg, in 1756. His father was an eminent musician, and the early proficiency of his son in music was almost incredible. He began the piano at three years of age; and from this period lost all pleasure in his other amusements. His taste was so scientific that he would spend his time in looking for thirds, and felt charmed with their harmony. At five years old, he began to compose little pieces, of such ingenuity that his father wrote them down.

He was a creature of universal sensibility, a natural enthusiast—from his infancy fond, melancholy and tearful. When scarcely able to walk, his first question to his friends, who took him on their knee, was, whether they loved him; and a negative always made him weep. His mind was all alive; and whatever touched it, made it palpitate throughout. When he was taught the rudiments of arithmetic, the walls and tables of his bed-chamber were found covered with figures. But the piano was the grand object of his devotion.

At six years old, this singular child commenced, with his father, and sister two years older than himself, one of those musical tours common in Germany; and performed at Munich before the Elector, to the great admiration of the most musical court on the continent. His ear now signalized itself, by detecting the most minute irregularities in the orchestra. But its refinement was almost a disease; a discord tortured him; he conceived a horror of the trumpet, except as a single accompaniment, and suffered from it so keenly, that his father, to correct what he regarded as the effect of ignorant terror, one day desired a trumpet to be blown in his apartment. The child entreated him not to make the experiment; but the trumpet sounded. Young Mozart suddenly turned pale, fell on the floor, and was on the point of going into convulsions, when the trumpeter was sent out of the room.

When only seven years old, he taught himself the violin; and thus, by the united effort of genius and industry, mastered the most difficult of all instruments. From Munich, he went to Vienna, Paris, and London. His reception in the British metropolis was such as the curious give to novelty, the scientific to intelligence, and the great to what administers to stately pleasure. He was flattered, honored, and rewarded. Handel had then made the organ a favorite, and Mozart took the way of popularity. His execution, which on the piano had astonished the English musicians, was equally wonderful on the organ, and he overcame all rivalry. On his departure from England, he gave a farewell concert, of which all the symphonies were composed by himself. This was the career of a child nine years old.

With the strengthening of his frame, the acuteness of his ear became less painful; the trumpet had lost its terror for him at ten years old; and before he had completed that period, he distinguished the church of the Orphans, at Vienna, by the composition of a mass and a trumpet duet, and acted as director of the concert.

Mozart had travelled the chief kingdoms of Europe, and seen all that could be shown to him there, of wealth and grandeur. He had yet to see the empire of musical genius. Italy was an untried land, and he went at once to its capital. He was present at the performance of Handel's admirable chant, the Miserere, which seems then to have been performed with an effect unequalled since. The singers had been forbidden to give a copy of this composition. Mozart bore it away in his memory, and wrote it down. This is still quoted among musicians, as almost a miracle of remembrance; but it may be more truly quoted as an evidence of the power which diligence and determination give to the mind. Mozart was not remarkable for memory; what he did, others may do; but the same triumph is to be purchased only by the same exertion. The impression of this day lasted during Mozart's life; his style was changed; he at once adopted a solemn reverence for Handel, whom he called "The Thunderbolt," and softened the fury of his inspiration, by the taste of Boccherini. He now made a grand advance in his profession, and composed an opera, "Mithridates," which was played twenty nights at Milan.

Mozart's reputation was soon established, and he was liberally patronised by the Austrian court. The following anecdote shows the goodness of his heart, and the estimation in which he was held. One day, as he was walking in the suburbs of Vienna, he was accosted by a mendicant, of a very prepossessing appearance and manner, who told his tale of wo with such effect, as to interest the musician strongly in his favor; but the state of his purse not corresponding with the impulse of his humanity, he desired the applicant to follow him to a coffee-house. Here Mozart, drawing paper from his pocket, in a few minutes composed a minuet, which, with a letter, he gave to the distressed man, desiring him to take it to his publisher. A composition from Mozart was a bill payable at sight; and to his great surprise, the now happy beggar was immediately presented with five double ducats.

The time which Mozart most willingly employed in compositions, was the morning, from six or seven o'clock till about the hour of ten. After this, he usually did no more for the rest of the day, unless he had to finish some piece that was wanted. He however always worked irregularly. When an idea struck him, he was not to be drawn from it, even if he were in the midst of his friends. He sometimes passed whole nights with his pen in his hand. At other times, he had such a disinclination to work, that he could not complete a piece till the moment of its performance. It once happened, that he put off some music which he had engaged to furnish for a court concert, so long, that he had not time to write out the part he was to perform himself. The Emperor Joseph, who was peeping everywhere, happening to cast his eyes on the sheet which Mozart seemed to be playing from, was surprised to see nothing but empty lines, and said to him, "Where's your part?" "Here," said Mozart, putting his hand to his forehead.

The Don Giovanni of this eminent composer, which is one of the most popular compositions ever produced, was composed for the theatre at Prague, and first performed in that city in 1787. This refined and intellectual music was not at that time understood in Germany; a circumstance which Mozart seems to have anticipated, for, previous to its first representation, he remarked to a friend, "This opera is not calculated for the people of Vienna; it will be more justly appreciated at Prague; but in reality I have written it principally to please myself and my friends." Ample justice has however at length been rendered to this great production; it is heard with enthusiasm in nearly all the principal cities of that quarter of the globe where music is cultivated as a science—from the frozen regions of Russia, to the foot of Mount Vesuvius. Its praise is not limited by the common attributes of good musical composition; it is placed in the higher rank of fine poetry; for not only are to be found in it exquisite melodies and profound harmonies, but the playful, the tender, the pathetic, the mysterious, the sublime, and the terrible, are to be distinctly traced in its various parts.

The overture to this opera is generally esteemed Mozart's best effort; yet it was only composed the night previous to the first representation, after the general rehearsal had taken place. About eleven o'clock in the evening, when retired to his apartment, he desired his wife to make him some punch, and to stay with him, in order to keep him awake. She accordingly began to tell him fairy tales, and odd stories, which made him laugh till the tears came. The punch, however, made him so drowsy, that he could go on only while his wife was talking, and dropped asleep as soon as she ceased. The efforts which he made to keep himself awake, the continual alternation of sleep and watching, so fatigued him, that his wife persuaded him to take some rest, promising to awake him in an hour's time. He slept so profoundly that she suffered him to repose for two hours. At five o'clock in the morning, she awoke him. He had appointed the music copiers to come at seven, and by the time they arrived, the overture was finished. They had scarcely time to write out the copy necessary for the orchestra, and the musicians were obliged to play it without a rehearsal. Some persons pretend, that they can discover in this overture the passages where Mozart dropped asleep and those where he suddenly awoke again.

This great composer was so absorbed in music, that he was a child in every other respect. He was extremely apprehensive of death; and it was only by incessant application to his favorite study, that he prevented his spirits from sinking totally under the fears of approaching dissolution. At all other times he labored under a profound melancholy, during which he composed some of his best pieces, particularly his celebrated Requiem. The circumstances attending this were remarkable.

One day, when his spirits were unusually oppressed, a stranger, of a tall, dignified appearance, was introduced. His manners were grave and impressive. He told Mozart that he came from a person who did not wish to be known, to request that he would compose a solemn mass, as a requiem for the soul of a friend, whom he had recently lost, and whose memory he was desirous of commemorating by this imposing service. Mozart undertook the task, and engaged to have it completed in a month. The stranger begged to know what price he set upon his work; and immediately paying him one hundred ducats, he departed.

The mystery of this visit seemed to have a strong effect on the mind of the musician. He brooded over it for some time; and then suddenly calling for writing materials, began to compose with extraordinary ardor. This application, however, was more than his strength could support; it brought on fainting fits, and his increasing illness obliged him to suspend his work. "I am writing the requiem for myself," said he one day to his wife; "it will serve for my own funeral service;" and this impression never afterwards left him. At the expiration of the month, the mysterious stranger appeared, and demanded the requiem. "I have found it impossible," said Mozart, "to keep my word; the work has interested me more than I expected, and I have extended it beyond my first design. I shall require another month to finish it."

The stranger made no objection; but observing that for this additional trouble it was but just to increase the premium, laid down fifty ducats more, and promised to return at the time appointed. Astonished at his whole proceeding, Mozart ordered a servant to follow this singular personage, and, if possible, to find out who he was. The man, however, lost sight of him, and was obliged to return as he went. Mozart, now more than ever persuaded that he was a messenger from the other world, sent to warn him that his end was approaching, applied with fresh zeal to the requiem; and in spite of his exhausted state, both of body and mind, he completed it before the end of the month. At the appointed day, the stranger returned; the requiem was finished; but Mozart was no more! He died at Vienna, 1791, aged 35 years.

ELIHU BURRITT.

IN an address delivered by Governor Everett, before a Mechanics' Association, in Boston, 1837, he introduced a letter from Elihu Burritt, a native of Connecticut, and then a resident of Worcester, Massachusetts, of which the following is a copy:—

"I was the youngest of many brethren, and my parents were poor. My means of education were limited to the advantages of a district school, and those again were circumscribed by my father's death, which deprived me, at the age of fifteen, of those scanty opportunities which I had previously enjoyed.

"A few months after his decease, I apprenticed myself to a blacksmith in my native village. Thither I carried an indomitable taste for reading, which I had previously acquired through the medium of the society library,—all the historical works in which I had at that time perused. At the expiration of a little more than half my apprenticeship, I suddenly conceived the idea of studying Latin.

"Through the assistance of an elder brother, who had himself obtained a collegiate education by his own exertions, I completed my Virgil during the evenings of one winter. After some time devoted to Cicero, and a few other

Latin authors, I commenced the Greek: at this time it was necessary that I should devote every hour of daylight, and a part of the evening, to the duties of my apprenticeship.

"Still I carried my Greek grammar in my hat, and often found a moment, when I was heating some large iron, when I could place my book open before me against the chimney of my forge, and go through with *tupto*, *tupteis*, *tuptei*, unperceived by my fellow-apprentices. At evening I sat down, unassisted, to the Iliad of Homer, twenty books of which measured my progress in that language during the evenings of another winter.

"I next turned to the modern languages, and was much gratified to learn that my knowledge of Latin furnished me with a key to the literature of most of the languages of Europe. This circumstance gave a new impulse to the desire of acquainting myself with the philosophy, derivation, and affinity of the different European tongues. I could not be reconciled to limit myself in these investigations, to a few hours, after the arduous labors of the day.

"I therefore laid down my hammer, and went to New Haven, where I recited to native teachers, in French, Spanish, German, and Italian. I returned, at the expiration of two years, to the forge, bringing with me such books in those languages as I could procure. When I had read these books through, I commenced the Hebrew, with an awakened desire of examining another field; and, by assiduous application, I was enabled in a few weeks to read this language with such facility, that I allotted it to myself as a task to read two chapters in the Hebrew Bible before breakfast, each morning; this, and an hour at noon, being all the time that I could devote to myself during the day.

"After becoming somewhat familiar with this language, I looked around me for the means of initiating myself into the fields of Oriental literature; and, to my deep regret and concern, I found my progress in this direction hedged in by the want of requisite books. I began immediately to devise means of obviating this obstacle; and, after many plans, I concluded to seek a place as a sailor on board some ship bound to Europe, thinking in this way to have opportunities of collecting, at different ports, such works in the modern and Oriental languages as I found necessary for this object. I left the forge at my native place, to carry this plan into execution.

"I travelled on foot to Boston, a distance of more than a hundred miles, to find some vessel bound to Europe. In this I was disappointed; and, while revolving in my mind what steps next to take, I accidentally heard of the American Antiquarian Society, at Worcester. I immediately bent my steps toward this place. I visited the hall of the American Antiquarian Society, and found there, to my infinite gratification, such a collection in ancient, modern, and Oriental languages, as I never before conceived to be collected in one place; and, sir, you may imagine with what sentiments of gratitude I was affected, when, upon evincing a desire to examine some of these rich and rare works, I was kindly invited to unlimited participation in all the benefits of this noble institution.

"Availing myself of the kindness of the directors, I spent three hours daily at the hall, which, with an hour at noon, and about three in the evening, make up the portion of the day which I appropriate to my studies, the rest being occupied in arduous manual labor. Through the facilities afforded by this institution, I have added so much to my previous acquaintance with the ancient, modern, and Oriental languages, as to be able to read upwards of FIFTY of them with more or less facility."

This statement, however extraordinary it may seem, is well known to be but a modest account of Mr. Burritt's wonderful acquirements. He is still (1843) a practical blacksmith, yet he finds time to pursue his studies. Nor are his acquisitions his only merit. He has been frequently invited to deliver lectures before lyceums, and other associations, and in these he has displayed no small degree of eloquence and rhetorical power. As he is still a young man, we may venture to affirm that his history affords an instance of self-cultivation, which, having regard to all the circumstances, is without a parallel.

GEORGE MORLAND.

THIS eccentric man and clever artist was born in London, in 1763. He gave very early indications of genius, and when quite a child, used to draw objects on the floor, with the implements of his father, who was a painter, in crayons. He executed pictures of pencils, scissors, and other things of the kind, with so much perfection, that his father often mistook them for real ones, and stooped down to pick them up. Some of George's drawings, executed before he was five years old, were exhibited with great applause at the society of artists in London.

These and other evidences of talent rendered him a favorite child; his father saw the germs of excellence in his own art, and, at the age of fourteen, had him apprenticed to himself, for seven years, during which his application was incessant. His father appears to have been harsh, unfeeling and selfish, and to have thought more of obtaining money from the talents and exertions of his son, than of giving him such training as should insure his success in life.

During his apprenticeship, George was confined to an upper room, copying drawings or pictures, and drawing from plaster casts. Being almost entirely restricted from society, all the opportunities he had for amusement were obtained by stealth, and his associates were a few boys in the neighborhood. The means of enjoyment were obtained by such close application to his business, as secretly to produce a few drawings or pictures more than his father imagined he could complete in a given time. These he lowered by a string from the window of his apartment, to his youthful companions, by whom they were converted into money, which they spent in common when opportunities offered.

In this manner passed the first seventeen years of the life of George Morland; and to this unremitted diligence and application he was indebted for the extraordinary power he possessed over the implements of his art. Avarice, however, was the ruling passion of his father, and this was so insatiable, that he kept his son incessantly at work, and gave him little, if any, education, except as an artist. To this cause must doubtless be attributed the irregularities of his subsequent life.

Morland's earlier compositions were small pictures of two or three figures, chiefly from the ballads of the day. These his father put into frames and sold for from one to three guineas. They were remarkable for their simple truth, and were much admired. Many of them were engraved, and widely circulated, which gave the young artist an extensive reputation. About this time, he went to Margate to spend the summer, and, by the advice of a friend, commenced portrait painting there. Great numbers of fashionable persons came to sit to him, and he commenced several pictures.

But the society of accomplished people made him feel his own ignorance to such a degree as to render him unhappy, and he sought relief at pig races and in other coarse amusements, projected for the lower order of visitors at Margate. These at last engaged his whole attention, and the portraits were thrown aside, to be finished in town. He at last returned, with empty pockets and a large cargo of unfinished canvasses.

Morland continued, however, to rise rapidly in his profession, and he might easily have secured an ample fortune. The subjects he selected for his pencil, were, generally, rural scenes, familiar to every eye, and the sentiment they conveyed was felt by every beholder. Many of these were admirably engraved by the celebrated J. B. Smith, and immense numbers were sold. Morland now had demands for more pictures than he could execute, and at almost any price.

But, unhappily, this gifted artist had already become addicted to the society of low picture dealers, and other dissipated persons, and his habits were, consequently, exceedingly irregular. His chief pleasures seemed to be—a ride into the country to a grinning match, a jolly dinner with a drinking bout after it, and a mad scamper home with a flounce in the mud.

Such, at last, was Morland's dislike of the society of gentlemen, and his preference of low company, that he would not paint pictures for the former class, but preferred selling them to certain artful dealers, who were his associates, and who flattered his vices, so that they might prey upon his genius. Of these persons, who pretended to be his friends, he did not obtain more than half price for his paintings. This system was carried to such an extent that Morland was at last entirely cut off from all connection with the real admirers of his works. If a gentleman wished to get one of his pictures, he could only do it by employing one of these harpies who had access to the artist, and who would wheedle a picture out of him for a mere trifle, and all under the mask of friendship.

About the year 1790, Morland lived in the neighborhood of Paddington. At this period, he had reached the very summit of his professional fame, and also of his extravagance. He kept, at one time, no less than eight saddle horses at livery, at the sign of the White Lion, opposite to his house, and affected to be a good judge of horse-flesh. Frequently, horses, for which one day he would give thirty or forty guineas, he would sell the next, for less than half that sum; but as the honest fraternity of horse-dealers knew their man, and would take his note at two months, he could the more easily indulge this propensity, and appear, for a short time, in cash, until the day of payment came, when a picture was produced as a douceur for a renewal of the notes.

This was one source of calamity which neither his industry, for which he was not remarkable, nor his talents, were by any means adequate to overcome. His wine merchant, who was also a gentleman in the discounting line, would sometimes obtain a picture worth fifty pounds, for the renewal of a bill. By this conduct, he heaped folly upon folly, to such a degree, that a fortune of ten thousand a year would have proved insufficient for the support of his waste and prodigality.

Morland's embarrassments, which now crowded upon him, were far from producing any change in his conduct; and, at length, they conducted him, through the hands of a bailiff, into prison, of which, by the way, he had always entertained a foreboding apprehension. This, however, did not render him immediately unhappy, but rather afforded him an opportunity of indulging, without restraint of any kind, his fatal propensities. There, he could mingle with such companions as were best adapted to his taste, and there too, in his own way, he could, without check or control, reign or revel, surrounded by the very lowest of the vicious rabble.

When in confinement, and even sometimes when he was at liberty, it was common for him to have four guineas a day and his drink,—an object of no small consequence, as he began to drink before he began to paint, and continued to do both alternately, till he had painted as much as he pleased, or till the liquor had completely overcome him, when he claimed his money, and business was at an end for that day.

This laid his employer under the necessity of passing his whole time with him, in order to keep him in a state fit for labor, and to carry off the day's work when it was done; otherwise some eavesdropper snapped up his picture, and his employer was left to obtain what redress he could. By pursuing this fatal system, he ruined his health, enfeebled his genius, and sunk himself into general contempt. His constitution could not long sustain such an abuse of its powers. He was attacked with paralysis, and soon after, he died.

Thus perished George Morland, at the early age of forty-one years; a man whose best works will command esteem as long as any taste for the art of painting remains; one whose talents might have insured him happiness and distinction, if he had been educated with care, and if his entrance into life had been guided by those who were able and willing to caution him against the snares which are continually preparing by knavery for the inexperience and heedlessness of youth. Many of the subjects of Morland's pencil, are such as, of themselves, are far from pleasing. He delighted in representations of the pigsty. Yet even these, through the love we possess of truthful imitations, and the hallowing powers of genius, excite emotions of pleasure. His pictures of scenery around the cottage door, and of those rustic groups familiar to every eye, have the effect of poetry, and call into exercise those gentle sentiments, which, however latent, exist in every bosom. It is sad to reflect, that one who did so much to refine and civilize mankind, should himself have been the victim of the coarsest of vices.

WILLIAM PENN.

THIS remarkable man was born in the parish of St Catherine's, near the tower of London, on the 14th day of October, 1644. His father, who served in the time of the Commonwealth, in some of the highest maritime offices, was knighted by Charles the Second, and became a peculiar favorite of the then Duke of York.

Young Penn had good advantages for education, and made such early improvement, that, about the fifteenth year of his age, he was entered a student in Christ's Church College, Oxford, where he continued two years. He delighted much in manly sports at times of recreation; but at length, being influenced by an ardent desire after pure and spiritual religion, of which he had before received some taste through the ministry of Thomas Lee, one of the people denominated Friends, or Quakers, he, with certain other students of that University, withdrew from the national way of worship, and held private meetings for the exercise of religion. Here they both preached and prayed among themselves. This gave great offence to the heads of the college, and young Penn, being but sixteen years of age, was fined for non-conformity, and at length, for persevering in his peculiar religious practices, was expelled the college.

Having in consequence returned home, he still took great delight in the company of sober and religious people. His father, perceiving that this would be an obstacle in the way of his son's preferment, endeavored by words, and even very severe measures, to persuade him to change his conduct. Finding these methods ineffectual, he was at length so incensed, that he turned young William out of doors. The latter was patient under this trial, and at last the father's affection subdued his anger. He then sent his son to France, in company with some persons of quality that were making a tour thither.

He continued in France a considerable time, and, under the influence of those around him, his mind was diverted from religious subjects. Upon his return, his father, finding him not only a proficient in the French language, but also possessed of courtly manners, joyfully received him, hoping now that his point was gained. Indeed, some time after his return from France, his carriage was such as justly to entitle him to the character of a finished gentleman.

"Great about this time," says one of his biographers, "was his spiritual conflict. His natural inclination, his lively and active disposition, his father's favor, the respect of his friends and acquaintance, strongly pressed him to embrace the glory and pleasures of this world, then, as it were, courting and caressing him, in the bloom of youth, to accept them. Such a combined force seemed almost invincible; but the earnest supplication of his soul being to the Lord for preservation, He was pleased to grant such a portion of his power or spirit, as enabled him in due time to overcome all opposition, and with an holy resolution to follow Christ, whatsoever reproaches or persecutions might attend him."

About the year 1666, and when he was twenty-two years of age, his father committed to his care and management a considerable estate in Ireland, which occasioned his residence in that country. Thomas Lee, whom we have before mentioned, being at Cork, and Penn hearing that he was to be shortly at a meeting in that city, went to hear him; and by the preaching of this man, which had made some impression on his mind ten years before, he was now thoroughly and effectually established in the faith of the Friends, and afterwards constantly attended the meetings of that people. Being again at a meeting at Cork, he, with many others, was apprehended, and carried before the mayor, and, with eighteen of his associates, was committed to prison; but he soon obtained his discharge. This imprisonment was so far from terrifying, that it strengthened him in his resolution of a closer union with that people, whose religious innocence was the only crime for which they suffered. He now openly joined with the Quakers, and brought himself under the reproach of that name, then greatly ridiculed and hated. His former companions turned their caresses and compliments into bitter gibes and malignant derision.

His father, receiving information of what had passed, ordered him home; and the son readily obeyed. His deportment attested the truth of the information his father had received. He now again attempted, by every argument in his power, to move him; but finding it impossible to obtain a general compliance with the customs of the times, he would have borne with him, provided he would have taken off his hat, in the presence of the king, the duke of York, and himself.

This being proposed to the son, he desired time to consider of it. His father, supposing this to be with an intention of consulting his friends, the Quakers, assured him that he should see the face of none of them, but retire to his chamber till he could return him an answer. "Accordingly he withdrew, humbling himself before God, with fasting and supplication, to know his heavenly mind and will, and became so strengthened in his resolution, that, returning to his father, he humbly signified that he could not comply with his desire."

All endeavors proving ineffectual to shake his constancy, his father, seeing himself utterly disappointed in his hopes, again turned him out of doors. After a considerable time, his steady perseverance evincing his integrity, his father's wrath became somewhat abated, so that he winked at his return to, and continuance with, his family; and though he did not publicly seem to countenance him, yet, when imprisoned for being at meetings, he would privately use his interest to get him released. In the twenty-fourth year of his age, he became a minister among the Quakers, and continued his useful labors, inviting the people to that serenity and peace of conscience he himself witnessed, till the close of his life.

A spirit warmed with the love of God, and devoted to his service, ever pursues its main purpose; thus, when restrained from preaching, Penn applied himself to writing. The first of his publications appears to have been entitled "Truth Exalted." Several treatises were also the fruits of his solitude, particularly the one entitled "No Cross, no Crown."

In the year 1670, came forth the Conventicle Act, prohibiting Dissenters' meetings, under severe penalties. The edge of this new weapon was soon turned against the Quakers, who, not accustomed to flinch in the cause of religion, stood particularly exposed. Being forcibly kept out of their meeting-house in Grace Church street, they met as near it, in the open street, as they could: and Penn, preaching there, was apprehended, and committed to Newgate. At the next sessions of the Old Bailey, together with William Mead, he was indicted for "being present at, and preaching to, an unlawful, seditious, and riotous assembly." At his trial he made a brave defence, discovering at once both the free spirit of an Englishman and the undaunted magnanimity of a Christian, insomuch that, notwithstanding the frowns and menaces of the bench, the jury acquitted him.

Not long after this trial, and his discharge from Newgate, his father died, perfectly reconciled to his son, and left him both his paternal blessing, and an estate of fifteen hundred pounds a year. He took leave of his son with these remarkable words: "Son William, if you and your friends keep to your plain way of preaching, and keep to your plain way of living, you will make an end of the priests to the end of the world. Bury me by my mother; live all in love; shun all manner of evil; and I pray God to bless you all; and he will bless you."

In February, 1670, Penn was preaching at a meeting in Wheeler street, Spitalfields, when he was pulled down, and led out by soldiers into the street, and carried away to the Tower, by order of Sir John Robinson, lieutenant of the Tower. He was examined before Sir John and several others, and then committed, by their orders, to Newgate, for six months. Being at liberty at the expiration of that time, he soon after went to Holland and Germany, where he zealously endeavored to propagate the principles of the Quakers.

In March, 1680, he obtained from Charles II. a grant of the territory which now bears the name of Pennsylvania. This was in compensation of a crown debt due to his father. Having previously published an account of the province, inviting emigrants to accompany him thither, he set sail in June, 1682, with many friends, especially Quakers, and after a prosperous voyage of six weeks, they came within sight of the American coast. Sailing up the river Delaware, they were received by the inhabitants with demonstrations of joy and satisfaction. Having landed at Newcastle, a place mostly inhabited by the Dutch, Penn next day summoned the people to the court-house, where possession of the country was legally given him.

Having invited the Indians to meet him, many chiefs and persons of distinction, appointed to represent them, came to see him. To these he gave several valuable presents, the produce of English manufactures, as a testimony of that treaty of amity and good understanding, which, by his benevolent disposition, he ardently wished to establish with the native inhabitants. He made a most favorable impression upon the savages, and thus secured to Pennsylvania their favor. He then more fully stated the purpose of his coming, to the people, and the benevolent object of his government, giving them assurances of the free enjoyment of liberty of conscience in things spiritual, and of perfect civil freedom in matters temporal. He recommended to them to live in sobriety and peace one with another. After about two years residence in the country, all things being in a thriving and prosperous condition, he returned to England; and James II. coming soon after to the throne, he was taken into favor by that monarch, who, though a bigot in religion, was nevertheless a friend to toleration.

At the revolution, being suspected of disaffection to the government, and looked upon as a Papist or a Jesuit, under the mask of a Quaker, he was examined before the Privy Council, Dec., 1688; but, on giving security, was discharged. In 1690, when the French fleet threatened a descent on England, he was again examined before the council, upon an accusation of corresponding with King James, and was held to bail for some time, but was released in Trinity Term. He was attacked a third time the same year, and deprived of the privilege of appointing a governor for Pennsylvania; till, upon his vindication, he was restored to his right of government. He designed now to go over a second time to Pennsylvania, and published proposals in print for another settlement there; when a fresh accusation appeared against him, backed by one William Fuller, who was afterwards declared by parliament to be a notorious imposter. A warrant was granted for Penn's apprehension, which he narrowly escaped at his return from the funeral of George Fox, the founder and head of the Quakers. He now concealed himself for two or three years, and during this recess, wrote several pieces. At the end of 1693, through the interest of Lord Somers and others, he was allowed to appear before the king and council, when he represented his innocence so effectually that he was acquitted.

In 1699, he again went out to Pennsylvania, accompanied by his family, and was received by the colonists with demonstrations of the most cordial welcome. During his absence, some persons endeavored to undermine the American proprietary governments, under pretence of advancing the prerogative of the crown, and a bill for that purpose was brought into the H. of Lords. Penn's friends, the proprietors and adventurers then in England, immediately represented the hardships of their case to the parliament, soliciting time for his return, to answer for himself, and accordingly pressing him to come over as soon as possible. Seeing it necessary to comply, he summoned an assembly at Philadelphia, to whom, Sept. 15th, 1701, he made a speech, declaring his reasons for leaving them; and the next day he embarked for England, where he arrived about the middle of December. After his return, the bill, which, through the solicitations of his friends, had been postponed the last session of parliament, was wholly laid aside.

In the year 1707, he was unhappily involved in a suit at law with the executors of a person who had been formerly his steward, against whose demands he thought both conscience and justice required his endeavors to defend himself. But his cause, though many thought him aggrieved, was attended with such circumstances, that the court of chancery did not think it proper to relieve him; wherefore he was obliged to dwell in the Old Bailey, within the rules of the Fleet, some part of this and the ensuing year, until such time as the matter in dispute was accommodated.

In the year 1710, the air of London not agreeing with his declining constitution, he took a seat at Rushcomb, in Buckinghamshire. Here he experienced three successive shocks of apoplexy in 1712, the last of which sensibly impaired his memory and his understanding. His religious zeal, however, never abated, and up to 1716, he still frequently went to the meeting at Reading. Two friends calling upon him at this time, although very weak, he expressed himself sensibly, and when they were about to take leave of him, he said, "My love is with you; the Lord preserve you, and remember me in the Everlasting Covenant."

After a life of ceaseless activity and usefulness, Penn closed his earthly career on the 13th of May, 1718, in the seventy-sixth year of his age. He was buried at Jourdans, in Buckinghamshire, where several of his family had been interred.

JOHN SMITH.

THERE are few names that excite more interest or awaken more romantic associations than that of Captain John Smith. He passed through a series of the most remarkable events in Europe; and coming to our country at a period which was favorable to the exercise of his peculiar genius, he became the hero of many stirring adventures.

He was born at Willoughby, in the county of Lincolnshire, England, in the year 1579, and was descended from an ancient family. He displayed a love of enterprise in his early childhood, and he says that at thirteen years old he was "set upon brave adventures." This disposition led him to dispose of his books, his satchel, and what other little property he had, for the purpose of raising money to take him to sea; but losing his parents about this time, he received from them a considerable fortune. He was now induced to change his plans, and became apprenticed to an eminent merchant in London.

As might be expected, the drudgery and confinement of a compting house were very distasteful to one who was bent upon adventure; accordingly, with but ten shillings in his pocket, he became a follower of the son of Lord Willoughby, who was going to France. When he arrived there, he went into the service of Captain Joseph Duxbury, with whom he remained four years in Holland. How he was occupied during this period is uncertain. About this time, a Scotch gentleman kindly gave him some money, and letters to Scotland, assuring him of the favor of King James.

Smith now set sail, and arrived in Scotland after many disasters by sea, and great sickness of body. He delivered his letters, and was treated with kindness and hospitality; but his stay was short. Returning to his native town, and disappointed in not having found food for his wild love of adventure, he went into a forest, built himself a sort of hut, and studied military history and tactics. Here he lived for a time, being provided by his servant with the comforts of civilization, at the same time that he pleased his imagination with the idea of being a hermit. Accident throwing him into the society of an Italian gentleman, in military service, his ardor for active life was revived, and he set out again upon his travels, intending to fight against the Turks.

Being robbed of all his baggage and property in the Low Countries by some dastardly Frenchmen, he fortunately met with great kindness and generosity from several noble families. Prompted, however, by the same restless spirit with which he commenced life, he left those who were strongly interested in his welfare, and set out upon a journey, with a light purse and a good sword. In the course of his travels, he was soon in such a state of suffering from hunger and exposure, that he threw himself down in a wood, and there expected to die. But relief again appeared; a rich farmer chanced to come that way, who, upon hearing his story, supplied his purse, thus giving him the means of prosecuting his journey. There is scarcely an instance on record of a stranger receiving such kindness from his fellow-men, as did this same Smith.

He now went from port to port in search of a ship of war. During his rambles, he met, near a town in Brittany, with one of the villains who had robbed him. Smith immediately fought and vanquished him, making him confess his villany before a crowd of spectators. He then went to the seat of the Earl of Ployer, who gave him money, with which he embarked from

Marseilles for Italy, in a ship in which there was a number of Catholic pilgrims of various nations. A furious storm arising, these devotees took it into their heads that Heaven, in anger at the presence of a heretic, thus manifested its displeasure. They, therefore, set upon our hero, who, in spite of a valorous defence, was, like a second Jonah, thrown into the sea; but whether the angry elements were appeased by the offering, history saith not.

Being near the island of Saint Mary's, Smith easily swam thither, and was the next day taken on board a French ship, the commander of which, fortunately for Smith, was a friend of the Earl of Ployer, and treated him with great kindness. They then sailed to Alexandria, in Egypt. In the course of their voyage in the Levant, they met with a rich Venetian merchant ship, which, taking the French ship for a pirate, fired a broadside into her. This rough salutation, of course, brought on an engagement, in which the Venetians were defeated, and her cargo taken on board the victorious ship. Smith here met with something congenial to his wild and reckless spirit; and showing great valor on the occasion, he was rewarded with a large share of the booty. With this, he was enabled to travel in Italy, gratifying his curiosity by the interesting objects with which that country is filled. He at length set off for Gratz, the residence of Ferdinand, Archduke of Austria, and afterwards emperor of Germany.

The war was now raging between Rodolph, emperor of Germany, and Mahomet III., Grand Seignor of Turkey. Smith, by the aid of two of his countrymen, became introduced to some officers of distinction in the imperial army, who were very glad to obtain so valiant a soldier as Smith was likely to prove. This was in the year 1601. The Turkish army, under the command of Ibrahim Pasha, had besieged and taken a fortress in Hungary, and were ravaging the country. They were also laying siege to Olympach, which they had reduced to extremity.

Baron Kissel, who annoyed the besiegers from without, was desirous of sending a message to the commander of the garrison. Here was now an opportunity for Smith's talents and prowess to come into play. He entered upon his duty, and by means of telegraphs, he communicated the desired intelligence to the besieged fortress; and then, exercising his ingenuity, he arranged some thousands of matches on strings, so that when they were fired, the report deceived the Turks into the idea that a body of men were there. They consequently marched out to attack them. Smith's forces, with those of the garrison, which had been duly apprized of the scheme, fell upon them, and routed them. The Turks were now obliged to abandon the siege. This brilliant and successful exploit placed our hero at the head of a troop of two hundred and fifty horse, in the regiment of Count Meldritch.

The next adventure in which Smith's ingenuity was called into exercise was at the siege of Alba Regalis, in Hungary. He here contrived a sort of bomb, by which the Turks were greatly annoyed and their city set on fire; a bold military manœuvre being adopted at the critical moment, the place was taken, the Turks suffering great loss. A number of sieges and undecisive skirmishes now followed, which brought upon the Christians the jeers and scoffs of the Turks. One of their number, Lord Turbashaw, a man of military renown, sent a challenge to any captain of the Christian army to fight with him in single combat. The choice fell upon Smith, who ardently desired to meet the haughty Mussulman.

The day was appointed, the ground selected and lined with warlike soldiers and fair ladies. Lord Turbashaw entered the lists in splendid gilt armor, with wings on his shoulders, of eagle's feathers, garnished with gold and jewels. A janizary bore his lance, and two soldiers walked by the side of his horse. Smith was attended only by a page, bearing his lance. He courteously saluted his antagonist, and, at the sound of the trumpet, their horses set forward. They met with a deadly shock. Smith's lance pierced the visor of the Turk, and he fell dead from his horse. The day after, another challenge was sent to Smith; another encounter took place; and he was again victorious. Still another challenge met with the same result, and Smith was rewarded for his prowess in a signal manner, being made major of his regiment, and receiving all sorts of military honors. The Prince of Transylvania gave him a pension of three hundred ducats a year, and bestowed upon him a patent of nobility.

These events occurred about the year 1600. Various military movements followed in Moldavia, Smith taking an active part in whatever of enterprise and daring was going forward. In one instance, he narrowly escaped with his life.

In a mountainous pass, he was decoyed into an ambuscade, and though the christians fought desperately, they were nearly all cut to pieces. Smith was wounded and taken, but his life was spared by the cupidity of the conquerors, who expected a large sum for his ransom. He was sold as a slave and sent to Constantinople. He was afterwards removed to Tartary, where he suffered abuse, cruelty, and hardships of every description. At last he seized a favorable opportunity, rose against his master, slew him, clothed himself in his dress, mounted his horse, and was again at liberty.

Roaming about in a vast desert for many days, chance at length directed him to the main road, which led from Tartary to Russia, and in sixteen days he arrived at a garrison, where the governor and his lady took off his irons and treated him with great care and kindness. Thence he travelled into Transylvania, where he arrived in 1603. Here he met many of his old companions in arms, who overwhelmed him with honors and attentions. They had thought him dead, and rejoiced over him as one risen from the grave.

Still unsatisfied with perils and honors, hearing that a civil war had broken out in Barbary, he sailed to Africa, but, not finding the cause worthy of his sword, he returned to England in 1604, where a new field of adventure opened before him. Attention had been awakened in England upon the subject of colonizing America, by the representation of Captain Gosnold, who, in 1602, had made a voyage to the coast of New England. He gave delightful accounts of the fertility of the country and salubrity of the climate, and was anxious to colonize it. Of course, this plan was embraced with ardor by Smith, being a project just suited to his roving disposition, and his love for "hair breadth 'scapes."

James I., who was now king, being inclined to the plan, an expedition was fitted out in 1606, of one hundred and five colonists, in three small vessels. Among the foremost of the adventurers were Gosnold and Smith, who seemed to be drawn together by a kind of instinct. After a voyage of four months, in which dissensions and mutiny caused much trouble and uneasiness, and which resulted in Smith's imprisonment during the voyage, the colonists arrived at Chesapeake Bay in April, 1607. The landscape, covered with the new grass of spring, and varied with hills and valleys, seemed like enchantment to the worn-out voyagers. With joy they left their ships, and passed many days in choosing a spot for a resting-place and a home.

Here new troubles assailed them. The Indians in the vicinity looked upon their encroachments with jealous eyes, and attacked them with their arrows, but the colonists quickly dispersed them with muskets. Others, however, more peaceable, treated our adventurers with kindness. A settlement was now made upon a peninsula on James's river, to which they gave the name of Jamestown.

Of course, in a settlement like this, there must be suffering, and consequently, discontent. Much of this was manifested towards Smith, who, by his energy and perseverance, excited the envy of those associated with him in the management of the infant colony. At the same time, he became the object of dread to the Indians, by his bravery and resources. Many of the colonists died of hunger and disease; many were dispirited; and at last, in despair, they turned to our adventurer as their only hope in this hour of need. Like all generous spirits, he forgot his injuries, and set himself to work to remedy the evils that beset them. By his ingenuity and daring, he obtained from the Indians liberal supplies of corn, venison, and wild fowl, and, under the influence of good cheer, the colonists became, comparatively, happy.

But a new and unforeseen calamity awaited our hero. Having penetrated into the country, with but few followers, he was beset by a large party of Indians, and, after a brave resistance, was taken prisoner. But the spirit and presence of mind of this remarkable man did not forsake him in this alarming crisis. He did not ask for life, for this would, probably, have hastened his death; but requesting that he might see the Indian chief, he at the same time drew from his pocket a compass, and directed attention to it, partly by signs and partly by words which he had learned. The curious instrument amused and surprised his savage captors, and averted, for a time, the fate that awaited him.

They soon, however, tied him to a tree, and prepared to shoot him with their arrows. Changing their plans suddenly, they led him in a procession to a village, where they confined him and fed him so abundantly, that Smith thought they were probably fattening him for food. After a variety of savage ceremonies, the Indians took him to Werowcomoco—the residence of Powhatan, a celebrated chief, of a noble and majestic figure, and a countenance bespeaking the severity and haughtiness of one whose nod is law.

Powhatan was seated on a throne, with one of his daughters on each side of him. Many Indians were standing in the hut, their skins covered with paint, and ornamented with feathers and beads. As Smith was brought bound into the room, there was a loud shout of triumph, which warned him that his last hour had arrived. They gave him water to wash, and food to eat, and then, holding a consultation, they determined to kill him. Two large stones were brought in and placed before the unbending chief. Smith was dragged forward, his head placed upon the stones, and the fatal club raised for the cruel deed.

But what stays the savage arm? A child of twelve or thirteen, Pocahontas by name, the chief's favorite child, melted by the pity that seldom moves the heart of her race, ran to our hero, clasped his head in her arms, laid herself down with him on the block, determined to share his fate. Surely, of the numberless acts of kindness and benevolence which had been showered at different times upon Smith, this transcended them all! Startled by the act, and perhaps sympathizing with the feelings of his child, Powhatan raised Smith from the earth, and in two days, sent him with twelve Indian guides to Jamestown, from which place he had been absent seven weeks.

Smith found the colony disheartened by his absence, and in want of provisions. These he procured from the Indians, bartering blue beads for corn and turkeys. A fire broke out about this time, and burned up many of the houses of the colony; this damage, however, Smith set about repairing— his patience and energy surmounting every evil.

In June, 1608, our adventurer, tired of his mode of life, set out, with fourteen others, to explore Chesapeake Bay and the Potomac river. They encountered many tribes of Indians, but Smith's boldness always averted their assaults; and his frank and open demeanor generally turned his enemies into friends. The party returned to Jamestown in July, when Smith was made the president of the colony.

He now made several expeditions, frequently meeting with adventures, and falling in with numerous tribes of Indians. He and his party had many skirmishes, and suffered considerably from the assaults of the savages; but Smith's sagacity and ingenuity rendered them comparatively harmless. He explored the whole of Chesapeake Bay, sailing nearly 3000 miles, in the space of three months.

About this time, an expedition arrived from the mother country, under Capt. Newport, whose object was to make discoveries, and as they were to pass through Powhatan's territories, it was thought best to secure his favor by various presents. Accordingly, a bed and hangings, a chair of state, a suit of scarlet clothes, a crown, and other articles, were presented to him with great ceremony. At his coronation, having been with difficulty persuaded by the English to kneel, the moment the crown touched his head, a volley was fired from the boats, which caused the newly-made monarch to start up with affright. By way of return for these honors, Powhatan generously presented Captain Newport with his old shoes and mantle!

Notwithstanding Smith's exertions in behalf of the colony, the council in England were constantly dissatisfied with him. But he did not allow anything to abate his zeal for the welfare of the colony under his command; even though they were harassed by the Indians, and suffering from sickness and privation, he still kept up his courage and energy. He entreated the managers in England to send them out mechanics and husbandmen, instead of the idle young gentlemen who had come with Newport, and took every step in his power to promote the prosperity of the settlement.

The colony being now in great want of supplies, Smith made many exertions to procure them, but the Indians refused to part with any more provisions. A great war of words ensued between Smith and Powhatan, which ended in hostilities, Smith endeavoring to take the latter prisoner. The Indians, in their turn, made preparations to attack the English by night. Of this, they were warned by Pocahontas, who continued her kind interpositions in favor of Smith.

Our hero had now experienced, it would seem, enough of adventure and peril to satisfy his desires. He often narrowly escaped with his life, for the Indians held him in dread, as one to whose prowess they were always obliged to yield, and whose address was always an overmatch for their own. If they suspected him of any hostile intentions towards them, they propitiated him by loads of provisions. To give some idea of this—Smith returned from one of his expeditions with two hundred pounds of deer's flesh, and four hundred and seventy-nine bushels of corn. But at length, growing weary of exertion, and of the animadversion of the English company, with trouble abroad, and mutiny and sickness at home, he returned to England in 1609.

From this period to 1614, little or nothing is known of him. At this date, we again find him, true to his nature, sailing with two ships to Maine, for the purpose of capturing whales and searching for gold. Failing in these expectations, Smith left his men fishing for cod, while he surveyed the coast, from Penobscot to Cape Cod, trafficking with the Indians for furs. He then returned to England, and gave his map to the king, Charles I., and requested him to change some of the barbarous names which had been given to the places discovered. Smith gave the country the name of New England. Cape Cod, the name given by Gosnold, on account of the number of cod-fish found there, was altered by King Charles to Cape James, but the old title has always been retained. With the modesty ever manifested by Smith, he gave his own name only to a small cluster of islands, which, by some strange caprice, are now called the Isles of Shoals.

In January, 1615, Captain Smith set sail for New England, with two ships, from Plymouth in England, but was driven back by a storm. He embarked again in June, but met with all kinds of disasters, and was at last captured by a French squadron, and obliged to remain all summer in the admiral's ship. When this ship went to battle with English vessels, Smith was sent below; but when they fell in with Spanish ships, they obliged him to fight with them. They at length carried him to Rochelle, where they put him on board a ship in the harbor. This was but a miserable existence to our hero, and he sought various opportunities of escape.

At length, a violent storm arising, all hands went below, to avoid the pelting rain, and Smith pushed off in a boat, with a half pike for an oar, hoping to reach the shore. But a strong current carried him out to sea, where he passed twelve hours in imminent danger, being constantly covered with the spray. At last, he was thrown upon a piece of marshy land, where some fowlers found him, nearly drowned. He was relieved and kindly treated at Rochelle, and soon returned to England.

While these adventures were happening to Smith, Pocahontas became attached to an English gentleman, of the name of Rolfe, having previously separated herself from her father. This would seem an unnatural step, were it not for the fact that she had a more tender and mild nature than that of her nation, and could not endure to see the cruelties practised against the English, in whom she felt so strong an interest. She was married in 1613, and by means of this event a lasting peace was established with Powhatan and his tribe.

In 1616, Pocahontas visited England with her husband. She had learned to speak English well, and was instructed in the doctrines of Christianity. As soon as Smith heard of her arrival, he went immediately to see her, and he describes her in this interview as "turning about and obscuring her face," no doubt, overcome by old recollections. She afterwards, however, held a long conversation with Smith. This interesting creature was not destined to return to her own land, for, being taken sick at Gravesend, in 1617, she died, being only twenty-two years old.

Much has been written concerning this friend of the whites, and all agree in ascribing to her character almost every quality that may command respect and esteem. She combined the utmost gentleness and sweetness, with great decision of mind and nobleness of heart. Captain Smith has immortalized her by his eloquent description of her kindness to him and his people. From her child are descended some honorable families now living in Virginia.

Captain Smith intended to sail for New England in 1617, but his plans failed, and he remained in England, using constant exertions to persuade his countrymen to settle in America. In 1622, the Indians made a dreadful massacre at Jamestown, destroying three hundred and forty-seven of the English settlers. This news affected Smith very much, and he immediately made proposals to go over to New England, with forces sufficient to keep the Indians in check. But the people of England made so many objections to the plan, that it was given up by our hero, though with great regret. From this period, his story is little known, and we are only told that he died in 1631. His life is remarkable for the variety of wild adventures in which he was engaged; his character is marked as well by courage and daring, as by the somewhat opposite qualities of boldness and perseverance. He seems also to have possessed many noble and generous qualities of heart. He had, indeed, the elements of greatness, and had he been called to a wider field of action, he might have left a nobler fame among the annals of mankind.

ETHAN ALLEN.

THIS extraordinary man was born at Litchfield, or Salisbury, Connecticut, about the year 1740. He had five brothers and two sisters, named Heman, Heber, Levi, Zimri, Ira, Lydia and Lucy. Four or five of the former emigrated to Vermont, with Ethan, where their bold, active and enterprising spirits found an abundant opportunity for its display. Many a wild legend, touching their adventures, still lingers among the traditions of the Green Mountains.

About the year 1770, a dispute between New York and New Hampshire, as to the dividing line between the two provinces, and which had long been pending, came to a crisis. The territory of Vermont was claimed by both parties; and some of the settlers who had received grants from Governor Wentworth, of New Hampshire, were threatened with being ejected from their lands by legal processes, proceeding from the province of New York.

The Allens had selected their lands in the township of Bennington, which had now become a considerable place. The New York government, in conformity with their interpretation of their rights, had proceeded to grant patents, covering these very lands on which farms had now been brought to an advanced state of culture, and where houses had been built and orchards planted by the original purchasers. These proprietors were now called upon to take out new patents, at considerable expense, from New York, or lose their estates.

This privilege of purchasing their own property was regarded by the Vermonters as rather an insult, than a benefit, and most of them refused to comply. The question was at last brought to trial at Albany, before a New York court, Allen being employed by the defendants as their agent. The case was, of course, decided against them, and Allen was advised, by the king's attorney-general, to go home and make the best terms he could with his new masters, remarking, that "might generally makes right." The reply of the mountaineer was brief and significant: "The gods of the valley are not the gods of the hills;" by which he meant that the agents of the New York government would find themselves baffled at Bennington, should they undertake to enforce the decision of the court, against the settlers there.

Allen's prediction was prophetic. The sheriffs sent by the government were resisted, and finally, a considerable force was assembled, and placed under the command of Allen, who obliged the officers to desist from their proceedings. A proclamation was now issued by the governor of New York, offering a reward of twenty pounds for the apprehension of Allen. The latter issued a counter proclamation, offering a reward of five pounds to any one who would deliver the attorney-general of the colony into his power.

Various proceedings took place, and for several years, the present territory of Vermont presented a constant series of disturbances. The New York government persevered in its claims, and the settlers as obstinately resisted. In all these measures, whether of peace or war, Allen was the leader of the Green Mountain yeomanry. Various plots were laid for his apprehension, but his address and courage always delivered him from the impending danger. At last, the revolution broke out, and the dispute was arrested by events which absorbed the public attention. The rival claims being thus suspended, the people of Vermont were left to pursue their own course.

A few days after the battle of Lexington, a project was started at Hartford, Connecticut, for the capture of Fort Ticonderoga, then belonging to the British. Several persons set out upon this enterprise, and taking Bennington in their way, Allen joined them with some of his "Green Mountain Boys," and was appointed commander of the expedition. The little band arrived, without molestation, on the banks of Lake George, opposite the fort. They procured boats sufficient to carry eighty-three men. These crossed in the night, and landed just at the dawn of day. While the boats were gone back with the remainder of the troops, Allen resolved to attack the fort.

He drew up the men in three ranks, addressed them in a short harangue, ordered them to face to the right, and placing himself at the head of the middle file, led them silently, but with a quick step, up the heights where the fortress stood; and before the sun rose, he had entered the gate, and formed his men on the parade between the barracks. Here they gave three huzzas, which aroused the sleeping inmates. When Colonel Allen passed the gate, a sentinel snapped his fusee at him, and then retreated under a covered way. Another sentinel made a thrust at an officer with a bayonet, which slightly wounded him. Colonel Allen returned the compliment with a cut on the side of the soldier's head, at which he threw down his musket, and asked quarter.

No more resistance was made. Allen now demanded to be shown to the apartment of Captain Delaplace, the commander of the garrison. It was pointed out, and Allen, with Beman, his guide, at his elbow, hastily ascended the stairs, which were attached to the outside of the barracks, and called out with a voice of thunder at the door, ordering the astonished captain instantly to appear, or the whole garrison should be sacrificed.

Startled at so strange and unexpected a summons, the commandant sprang from his bed and opened the door, when the first salutation of his boisterous and unseasonable visitor was an order immediately to surrender the fort. Rubbing his eyes, and trying to collect his scattered senses, the captain asked by what authority he presumed to make such a demand. "In the name of the Great Jehovah, and the Continental Congress!" said Allen.

Not accustomed to hear much of the continental congress in this remote corner, nor to respect its authority when he did, the commandant began to remonstrate; but Colonel Allen cut short the thread of his discourse, by lifting his sword over his head, and reiterating the demand for an immediate surrender. Having neither permission to argue, nor power to resist, Captain Delaplace submitted, ordering his men to parade, without arms, and the garrison was given up to the victors.[A]

The fruit of this victory was about fifty prisoners, with one hundred and twenty pieces of cannon, beside other arms and military stores. A few days after, the fort at Crown Point was taken, and some other successful enterprises were achieved. Allen obtained great credit by these performances.

In the following autumn, he was twice despatched into Canada, to engage the inhabitants to lend their support to the American cause. In the last of these expeditions, he formed a plan, in concert with Colonel Brown, to reduce Montreal. Allen, accordingly, crossed the river in September, 1775, at the head of one hundred and ten men, but was attacked, before Brown could join him, by the British troops, consisting of five hundred men, and, after a most obstinate resistance, was taken prisoner. The events of his captivity he himself has recorded in a narrative compiled after his release, in the most singular style, but apparently with great fidelity.

For some time he was kept in irons, and treated with much severity. He was sent to England as a prisoner, with an assurance that, on his arrival there, he would meet with the halter. During the passage, extreme cruelty was exercised towards him and his fellow-prisoners. They were all, to the number of thirty-four, thrust, handcuffed, into a small place in the vessel, not more than twenty feet square. After about a month's confinement in Pendennie castle, near Falmouth, he was put on board a frigate, January 8, 1776, and carried to Halifax. Thence, after an imprisonment of five months, he was removed to New York.

On the passage from Halifax to the latter place, he was treated with great kindness by Captain Smith, the commander of the vessel, and he evinced his gratitude by refusing to join in a conspiracy on board to kill the British captain and seize the frigate. His refusal prevented the execution of the plan. He remained at New York for a year and a half, sometimes in confinement, and sometimes at large, on parole.

In 1778, Allen was exchanged for Colonel Campbell, and immediately afterwards, repaired to the head quarters of General Washington, by whom he was received with much respect. As his health was impaired, he returned to Vermont, after having made an offer of his services to the commander-in-chief, in case of his recovery. His arrival in Vermont was celebrated by the discharge of cannon; and he was soon appointed to the command of the state militia, as a mark of esteem for his patriotism and military talents. A fruitless attempt was made by the British to bribe him to lend his support to a union of Vermont with Canada. He died suddenly at his estate at Colchester, February 13, 1789.

Allen was a man of gigantic stature, being nearly seven feet in height, and every way of relative proportions. He possessed undaunted courage, and blended bold enterprise with much sagacity. His early education was imperfect, but he was the master-spirit in the society among which he lived, and he exercised a powerful influence in laying the foundations of the state of Vermont. He was a sincere friend of his country, and did much in behalf of the revolution. When applied to by the rebel Shays, to become the leader of the insurrection in 1786, he rejected the proffer with indignation.

Allen was a man of great determination, and, living in the midst of turmoil, was somewhat reckless in his temper. While he held a military command, during the revolution, a notorious spy was taken and brought to his quarters. Allen immediately sentenced him to be hung at the end of two or three days, and arrangements were accordingly made for the execution. At the appointed time, a large concourse of people had collected around the gallows, to witness the hanging. In the mean time, however, it had been intimated to Allen that it was necessary to have a regular trial of the spy.

This was so obvious, that he felt compelled to postpone the execution of the culprit. Irritated, however, at this delay of justice, he proceeded to the gallows, and, mounting the scaffold, harangued the assembly somewhat as follows: "I know, my friends, you have all come here to see Rowley hanged, and, no doubt, you will be greatly disappointed to learn that the performances can't take place to-day. Your disappointment cannot be greater than mine, and I now declare that if you'll come here a fortnight from this day, Rowley shall be hung, or I will be hung myself."

The rude state of society in which Allen spent the greater part of his life was little calculated to polish his manners. Being at Philadelphia, before the election of General Washington as president, he was invited to dinner, by the general upon an occasion of some ceremony. He took his seat by the side of Mrs. Washington, and in the course of the meal, seeing some Spanish olives before him, he took one of them, and put it in his mouth. It was the first he had ever tasted, and, of course, his palate revolted. "With your leave, ma'am," said he, turning to Lady Washington, "I'll take this plaguy thing out of my mouth."

When Allen was in England, a prisoner, persons who had heard him represented as a giant in stature, and scarcely short of a cannibal in habits and disposition, came to see him, and gazed at him with mingled wonder and disgust. It is said, that, on one occasion, a tenpenny nail was thrown in to him, as if he were a wild animal. He is reported to have picked it up, and, in his vexation, to have bitten it in two. It is in allusion to this that Doctor Hopkins wrote,—

> "Lo, Allen 'scaped from British jails,
> His tushes broke by biting nails," &c.

But however rude were Allen's manners, he was a man of inflexible integrity. He was sued, upon a certain occasion, for a note of hand, which was witnessed by an individual residing at Boston. When the case came on for trial in one of the Vermont courts, the lawyer whom Allen had employed to manage it so as to get time, rose, and, for the purpose of securing this object, pleaded a denial of the signature.

It chanced that Allen was in the court-house at this moment, and hearing this plea, he strode across the court-room, and, while his eyes flashed with indignation, he spoke to the court as follows: "May it please your honors, that's a lie! I say I did sign that note, and I didn't employ Lawyer C****** to come here and tell a falsehood. That's a genuine note, and I signed it, please your honors, and I mean to pay it; all I want is to put it over till next court, when I expect to have money enough to meet it!" This speech gratified the opposing counsel so much, that he immediately consented to the delay which Allen desired.

Though Allen's education was limited, by reading and reflection he had acquired a considerable amount of knowledge. Presuming upon this, and guided by the eccentricity which marked his character, he ventured to assail the Christian religion, in a book entitled, "The Oracles of Reason." Though he here expressed belief in a God, and a future state of rewards and punishments, he rejected the Bible, and seemed to favor the Pythagorian doctrine of transmigration of souls. He entertained the idea that he was himself destined to reappear on earth in the condition of a great white horse! These absurdities show into what depths of folly a great man may be led, if he permit his self-conceit to involve him in the discussion of subjects beyond his grasp.

DAVID CROCKETT.

THIS individual was one of those remarkable characters, formed by the rough and adventurous circumstances of western life. His paternal grandfather and grandmother, who were of Irish descent, were murdered by the Creek Indians, in Tennessee. He had an uncle who was wounded at the same time, and remained in captivity with the savages for seventeen months. The subject of our memoir was born in 1786, on the banks of Nola-chucky river, he being the fifth son.

At this period, Tennessee was nearly a wilderness, and the forests were still, to a great extent, the dominion of the Indian and the wild beast. Brought up in this condition, his youthful imagination tinged by the tragic story of his ancestors, it was natural that our young hero should have become an early lover of those wild enterprises and hazardous adventures which belong to border life.

In the memoir with which Crockett has favored us, he gives an account of many events, some of which are not a little marvellous, though we have no reason to doubt their truth. The following will serve as a specimen of his style, as well as of the circumstances which attended his childhood. "Joseph Hawkins, who was a brother to my mother, was in the woods hunting for deer. He was passing near a thicket of brush, in which one of our neighbors was gathering some grapes, as it was in the fall of the year, and the grape season. The body of the man was hid by the brush, and it was only as he would raise his hand to pull the bunches, that any part of him could be seen. It was a likely place for deer; and my uncle, having no suspicion that it was any human being, but supposing the raising of the hand to be the occasional twitch of a deer's ear, fired at the lump, and as the devil would have it, unfortunately shot the man through the body. I saw my father draw a silk handkerchief through the bullet hole, and entirely through his body; yet, after a little while, he got well, as little as any one would have thought it. What became of him, or whether he is dead or alive, I don't know; but I reckon he didn't fancy the business of gathering grapes in an out-of-the-way thicket again."

When David was about eight years old, his father settled in Jefferson county, Tennessee, and opened a small tavern, chiefly for wagoners. He was poor, and his son says, "Here I remained with him, till I was twelve years old. About that time, you may *guess*, if you are a yankee, and *reckon*, if, like me, you belong to the backwoods, that I began to make my acquaintance with hard times, and plenty of them."

At this period, an old Dutchman, who was proceeding to Rockbridge, a distance of four hundred miles, stopped over night at his father's house. He had a large stock of cattle, and needing assistance, David was hired by him, and proceeded on foot the whole of the journey. He was expected to continue with the Dutchman, but his love of home mastered him, and taking his clothes in a bundle on his back, he stole away one night, and begged his way among the straggling settlements, till he reached his father's residence.

David was now sent to school; but at the end of four days he had a quarrel with one of his mates, and having scratched his face badly, he did not dare to go again. He therefore spent several days in the woods, during school hours, leaving his father to suppose he was at his lessons. When he found out, from the master, what David had done, he cut a hickory stick, and approached him in great wrath, intending to chastise him severely. The boy saw the danger, and fled. It was a tight race, but youth had the advantage. David escaped, hid himself in the woods for a time, and then, bidding adieu to his home, set forth upon his adventures.

Passing through a great variety of conditions, he at last reached Baltimore, and for the first time looked forth upon the blue ocean and the ships that navigate it. He had heard of these things, but he tells us, that until he actually saw them, he did not in his heart believe in their existence. It seems that his first sight of the sea excited in his bosom those deep, yet indescribable emotions, known only to those who have had experience like his own.

He set out at length to return to his father's house; but, owing to a variety of causes, it was three years before he reached it. It was evening when he came to the tavern, and he concluded to ask for lodging, and not make himself known, till he saw how the land lay. He gives an account of what followed, in these terms:—

"After a while, we were all called to supper: I went with the rest. We sat down to the table, and began to eat, when my eldest sister recollected me: she sprung up, ran and seized me around the neck, and exclaimed, 'Here is my lost brother!'

"My feelings at this time it would be vain and foolish for me to attempt to describe. I had often thought I felt before, and I suppose I had; but sure I am, I never had felt as I then did. The joy of my sisters, and my mother, and indeed of all the family, was such that it humbled me, and made me sorry that I hadn't submitted to a hundred whippings, sooner than cause so much affliction as they had suffered on my account. I found the family had never heard a word of me from the time my brother left me. I was now almost fifteen years old, and my increased age and size, together with the joy of my father, occasioned by my unexpected return, I was sure would secure me against my long-dreaded whipping; and so they did. But it will be a source of astonishment to many, who reflect that I am now a member of the American Congress—the most enlightened body of men in the world—that at so advanced an age, the age of fifteen, I did not know the first letter in the book."

The following passage, continuing the narrative, evinces sense and feeling, which are honorable to our hero's head and heart. "I had remained for some short time at home with my father, when he informed me that he owed a man, whose name was Abraham Wilson, the sum of thirty-six dollars; and that if I would set in and work out the note, so as to lift it for him, he would discharge me from his service, and I might go free. I agreed to do this, and went immediately to the man who held my father's note, and contracted with him to work six months for it. I set in, and worked with all my might, not losing a single day in the six months. When my time was out, I got my father's note, and then declined working with the man any longer, though he wanted to hire me mighty bad. The reason was, it was a place where a heap of bad company met to drink and gamble, and I wanted to get away from them, for I knowed very well if I staid there I should get a bad name, as nobody could be respectable that would live there. I therefore returned to my father, and gave him up his paper, which seemed to please him mightily, for, though he was poor, he was an honest man, and always tried mighty hard to pay off his debts.

"I next went to the house of an honest old Quaker, by the name of John Kennedy, who had removed from North Carolina, and proposed to hire myself to him, at two shillings a day. He agreed to take me a week on trial, at the end of which he appeared pleased with my work, and informed me that he held a note on my father for forty dollars, and that he would give me that note if I would work for him six months. I was certain enough that I should never get any part of the note; but then I remembered it was my father that owed it, and I concluded it was my duty, as a child, to help him along, and ease his lot as much as I could. I told the Quaker I would take him up at his offer, and immediately went to work. I never visited my father's house during the whole of this engagement, though he lived only fifteen miles off. But when it was finished, and I had got the note, I borrowed one of my employer's horses, and, on a Sunday evening, went to pay my parents a visit. Some time after I got there, I pulled out the note, and handed it to my father, who supposed Mr. Kennedy had sent it for collection. The old man looked mighty sorry, and said to me he had not the money to pay it, and didn't know what he should do. I then told him I had paid it for him, and it was then his own; that it was not presented for collection, but as a present from me. At this, he shed a heap of tears; and as soon as he got a little over it, he said he was sorry he couldn't give me anything, but he was not able, he was too poor."

David continued to work for the Quaker, during which time he became enamored of a girl in the vicinity, and when he was eighteen he engaged to marry her; she, however, proved faithless, and wedded another man. The youth took it much to heart, and observes, "I now began to think that in making me, it was entirely forgotten to make my mate; that I was born odd, and should always remain so." He, however, recovered, and paid his addresses to a little girl of the neighborhood, whom he met one day when he had got lost in the woods, and married her. She had for her marriage portion two cows and two calves; and, with fifteen dollars' worth of furniture, they commenced house-keeping. He rented a small farm, and went to work. After a few years, he removed to another part of the state, where there was plenty of game, in consequence of which he became a hunter. About the year 1810, he settled on Bear Creek, where he remained till after the war of 1812.

During the Creek war in Tennessee, in 1812, Crockett served as a private soldier under General Jackson, and displayed no small share of enterprise and daring. He also served in one of the expeditions to Florida, meeting with a great variety of adventures. Soon after the close of the war, in 1815, he lost his wife, but married again, and, as he says, "went ahead."

After a time, he removed, with his family, to Shoal Creek, where the settlers, living apart from the rest of the world, set up a government for themselves; they established certain laws, and Crockett was elected one of the magistrates. The operations of this forest republic are thus described by our hero:—

"When a man owed a debt, and wouldn't pay it, I and my constable ordered our warrant, and then he would take the man, and bring him before me for trial. I would give judgment against him, and then an order for an execution would easily scare the debt out of him. If any one was charged with marking his neighbor's hogs, or with stealing anything,—which happened pretty often in those days,—I would have him taken, and if there was tolerable grounds for the charge, I would have him well whipped, and cleared. We kept this up till our legislature added us to the white settlements in Giles county, and appointed magistrates by law, to organize matters in the parts where I lived. They appointed every man a magistrate who had belonged to our corporation. I was then, of course, made a squire according to law, though now the honor rested more heavily on me than before. For, at first, whenever I told my constable, says I,—'Catch that fellow, and bring him up for trial,' away he went; and the fellow must come, dead or alive; for we considered this a good warrant, though it was only in verbal writings. But after I was appointed by the assembly, they told me my warrants must be in real writing, and signed; and that I must keep a book, and write my proceedings in it. This was a hard business on me, for I could just barely write my own name."

Crockett now rose rapidly; he was elected a colonel in the militia, and, by request of his friends, became a candidate for the state legislature. He made an electioneering tour of nearly three months, addressing the voters at various points. His account of this part of his life is full of wit; and not only throws much light upon western manners, but suggests many keen and sagacious reflections upon the character and conduct of political leaders, seeking the suffrages of the people. His success upon the stump was great, though he confesses he knew nothing about government, and dared not even touch the subject. He told droll stories, however, which answered a better purpose, and in the result, was triumphantly elected. We must not omit to give Crockett's own account of himself at this period.

"A short time after this," says he, "I was in Pulaski, where I met with Colonel Polk, now a member of Congress from Tennessee. He was at that time a member elected to the legislature, as well as myself; and in a large company he said to me, 'Well, Colonel, I suppose we shall have a radical change of the judiciary at the next session of the legislature.' 'Very likely, sir,' says I; and I put out quicker, for I was afraid some one would ask me what the judiciary was; and if I knowed, I wish I may be shot. I don't indeed believe I had ever before heard that there was any such thing in all nature; but still I was not willing that the people there should know how ignorant I was about it. When the time for meeting of the legislature arrived, I went on, and before I had been there long, I could have told what the judiciary was, and what the government was too; and many other things that I had known nothing about before."

Crockett now removed to the borders of the Obion, and settled in the woods, his nearest white neighbor being seven miles off. The country around gradually became peopled, and in the course of a few years he was again put in nomination, without his own consent or knowledge, for the legislature. His antagonist was Dr. Butler, a relative of General Jackson's, and, as Crockett describes him, "a clever fellow, and the most talented man I ever run against, for any office." Two other candidates were in the field, but David beat them all by a handsome majority. This occurred in 1825. In 1827, he was elected to Congress, and re-elected in 1829, by a majority of 3500 votes. No man could at that time stand against him, with hopes of success. In 1831, however, he lost his election, but succeeded in 1833. He was defeated in 1835, and, having gone to Texas, engaged in the defence of Bexar, and was slain in the storming of that place, March 6th, 1836.

The character of David Crockett is by no means to be set up as a model for imitation, yet he was a man of excellent traits of character. Brave, hospitable, honest, patriotic, and sincere, he was the representative of the hardy hunters of the west—a race of men fast fading away, or receding with the remote borders of our western settlements. Destitute of school education, he supplied the defect, in a great degree, by ready wit, and that talent which is developed strongly by the necessities of a hard and hazardous course of life. In civilized society, he retained the marks of his forest breeding, as well as the innate eccentricity of his character, and became conspicuous as one of those humorists, whom nothing can change from their original conformation.

DANIEL BOONE.

THERE are few names in the West better known, or more respected, than that of Colonel Daniel Boone. He is regarded as the founder of Kentucky, and in his character, was a good specimen of the early settler, who united in his own person the offices of hunter and husbandman, soldier and statesman. He was born in Pennsylvania, in the year 1746, and in his boyhood gave earnest of his future career, by his surpassing skill in the use of a gun, as exercised against squirrels, raccoons, and wild-cats.

A love of hunting became his ruling passion, and he would wander, for whole days alone, through the woods, seeming to take great delight in these rambles, even if he found no game. One morning, when he was about fourteen years old, he was observed, as usual, to throw the band that suspended his shot bag, over the shoulder, and go forth, accompanied by his dog. Night came, but, to the astonishment and alarm of his parents, the boy came not. Another day and another night passed, and still he did not return. The nearest neighbors, sympathizing with the distressed parents, who considered him lost, at length turned out, to aid in finding him.

After a long and weary search, a smoke was seen arising from a temporary hovel of sods and branches, at a distance of a league from any plantation, in which the astonished father found his child; he was, apparently, most comfortably occupied in making an experiment in housekeeping. Numerous skins of wild animals were stretched upon his cabin, as trophies of his hunting prowess. Ample fragments of their flesh were around—either thrown aside or prepared for cookery.

A few years after this, Boone removed, with his father, to North Carolina, where they founded a settlement upon the banks of the Yadkin. The country was new, and almost totally uninhabited; the game was abundant, and afforded ample scope for young Boone's talents as a hunter. One night, he went out with a friend, upon what is called a *fire hunt*, the object of which was to shoot deer. In this sport, an iron pan, filled with blazing knots of pitch pine, is carried by one of the sportsmen. This casts a ruddy glare deep into the forest; and the deer, as if bound by a spell of enchantment, stands still, and gazes at the unwonted apparition. The lustrous eye of the animal is easily seen by the hunter, and thus becomes a mark for the rifle.

On the present occasion, the two hunters had reached the corner of a farmer's field early in the evening, when Boone's companion, who held the fire pan, gave the signal that he *shined* the eyes of a deer. Boone approached with his ready rifle, and, perceiving the glistening eyes, was about to fire, when the deer suddenly retreated. He pursued, and, after a rapid chase through the woods, came suddenly out at the farmer's house. What was the young hunter's astonishment then to discover that the object upon which he had levelled his rifle a few minutes before, was a beautiful girl of sixteen, and the daughter of the farmer! Boone could do no less than enter the house. The scene that followed is thus described by the biographer:

"The ruddy, flaxen-haired girl stood full in view of her terrible pursuer, leaning upon his rifle, and surveying her with the most eager admiration. 'Rebecca, this is young Boone, son of our neighbor,' was the laconic introduction, offered by the father. Both were young, beautiful, and at the period when the affections exercise their most energetic influence. The circumstances of the introduction were favorable to the result, and the young hunter felt that the eyes of the deer had *shined* his bosom as fatally as his rifle-shot had ever done the innocent deer of the thickets.

"She, too, when she saw the high, open, bold forehead—the clear, keen, yet gentle and affectionate eye—the firm front, and the visible impress of decision and fearlessness of the hunter; when she interpreted a look, which said, as distinctly as looks could say it, 'how terrible it would have been to have fired!' she can hardly be supposed to have regarded him with indifference. Nor can it be wondered at that she saw in him her *beau ideal* of excellence and beauty.

"The inhabitants of cities, who live in splendid mansions, and read novels stored with unreal pictures of life and the heart, are apt to imagine that love, with all its golden illusions, is reserved exclusively for them. It is a most egregious mistake. A model of ideal beauty and perfection is woven in almost every youthful heart, of the finest and most brilliant threads that compose the web of existence. It may not be said that this forest maiden was deeply and foolishly smitten at first sight. All reasonable time and space were granted to the claims of maidenly modesty. As for Boone, he was incurably wounded by her, whose eyes he had *shined*, and as he was remarkable for the backwoods' attribute of never being beaten out of his track, he ceased not to woo, until he gained the heart of Rebecca Bryan. In a word, he courted her successfully, and they were married."

Boone removed with his wife to the head waters of the Yadkin, where he remained for several years, engaged in the quiet pursuits of a husbandman. But in process of time, the country was settled around him, and the restraints of orderly society became established. These were disagreeable to his love of unbounded liberty, and he began to think of seeking a new home in the yet unoccupied wilderness. Having heard an account of Kentucky from a man by the name of Finley, who had made an expedition thither, he determined to explore the country. Accordingly, in 1769, he set out with four associates, and soon, bidding adieu to the habitations of man, plunged into the boundless forest.

They ascended and crossed the Alleganies, and at last stood on the western summit of the Cumberland Ridge. What a scene opened before them!—the illimitable forest, as yet unbroken by civilized man, and occupied only by savage beasts and more savage men. Yet it bore the marks of the highest fertility. Trees of every form, and touched with every shade of verdure, rose to an unwonted height on every side. In the distance, broad rivers flashed beneath the sun. How little did these hunters imagine that this noble country, within the compass of fifty years, was to be dotted with villages, and crowned with cities!

The party proceeded in their march. They met with an abundance of every species of game. The buffalo occupied the plains by thousands; and on one occasion, the whole party came near being crushed by a herd of these animals, that came rushing like a torrent across a prairie.

They spent the summer in the woods, and in December divided themselves into two parties, for the purpose of extending their means of observation. Boone and Stewart formed one division of the party. As they proceeded toward the Kentucky river, they were never out of sight of buffaloes, deer and wild turkeys. While they were one day leisurely descending a hill, the Indian yell suddenly broke upon their ears; a moment after, they were surrounded by savages, who sprung up from the cane-brakes around, and made them captives. Their hands were bound, and they were compelled to march, a long distance, to the Indian camp. On the second night, they escaped, and returned to the place where they expected to meet their former companions. These, it appears, had returned to Kentucky. That very day, however, Boone's brother arrived with a single companion, having made his way through the trackless forest, from his residence on the Yadkin.

The four adventurers now devoted themselves to hunting; but, one day, while they were out, Boone and Stewart, being separated from their companions, were attacked by Indians, and the latter was shot dead by an arrow. Boone, with some difficulty, escaped to the camp. A short time after this, the companion of the elder Boone wandered into the woods, and was lost. The two brothers sought for him with anxious care, and at last found traces of blood and fragments of his clothes in the vicinity of a place where they had heard the howling of wolves. There was little doubt that he had fallen a sacrifice to these terrible animals. Boone and his brother were now the only white men west of the mountains, yet their spirits were not damped by their condition or by the sad fate which had befallen their companions. They hunted by day; cooked their game, sat by their bright fires and sung the airs of their country at night. They also devoted much of their time to the preparation of a cabin for the approaching winter.

This came at length and passed away; but they were now in want of many things, especially ammunition, which was beginning to fail them. After long consultation, it was agreed that the elder Boone should return to North Carolina, and bring back ammunition, horses, and supplies.

The character of Daniel Boone, in consenting to be left alone in the wilderness, surrounded by perils from the Indians and wild beasts, of which he had so recently and terribly been made aware, appears in its true light. We have heard of a Robinson Crusoe, made so by the necessities of shipwreck; but all history can scarcely furnish another instance of a man, voluntarily consenting to be left alone among savages and wild beasts, seven hundred miles from the nearest white inhabitants.

The separation at last came. The elder brother disappeared in the forest, and Daniel Boone was left in the cabin, entirely alone. Their only dog followed the departing brother, and our hunter had nothing but his unconquerable spirit to sustain him during the long and lonely days and nights, visited by the remembrance of his distant wife and children.

To prevent the recurrence of dark and lonely thoughts, soon after his brother's departure, Boone set out on a tour of observation, and made an excursion to the Ohio river. He returned at last to his camp, which he found undisturbed. From this point he continued to make trips into the woods, in which he met with a variety of adventures. It was in May that his brother left him, and late in July he returned, with two horses and an abundant supply of needful articles. He brought also the welcome intelligence of the welfare of his brother's family and their kind remembrance of him.

The two brothers now set about selecting a situation for a settlement, where they intended to bring their families. One day, as they were passing through the woods, they saw a herd of buffaloes in great uproar. They were running, plunging, and bellowing, as if roused to fury. The hunters approached the throng, and perceived that a panther had leaped upon the back of one of these huge animals, and was gnawing away the flesh. The buffalo, maddened by the agony, dashed among the herd, and these were soon thrown into wild confusion. Boone picked his flint, took a deliberate aim, and fired; the panther fell from his seat, and the herd passed on.

We cannot pursue the history of our hero, in all its adventurous details. We have told enough to display the leading traits of his character, and we must now hasten on, only noting the principal events. He returned with his brother to North Carolina, and in September, 1773, commenced his removal to Kentucky, with his own family and five others, for the purpose of settling there. They were joined by forty men, who placed themselves under Boone's guidance. On their route they were attacked by the Indians; six of the men were killed, and the cattle were dispersed. The emigrants, therefore, returned as far as Clinch river, where they made a temporary settlement.

In 1775, Boone assisted in building a fort at a place which was called Boonesburgh, and when completed, he removed his family thither. Two years after, he here sustained two formidable sieges from the Indians, whom he repulsed. In the following year he was taken while hunting, by the savages, and carried to Detroit. He escaped, and at last returned to his family. Again the fort was invested by the Indians and Canadian Frenchmen, four hundred and fifty strong. Boone, with fifty men, held out, and finally the assailants withdrew. This was the last attack upon Boonesburgh.

In 1792, Kentucky was admitted into the Union as a state, and soon after, Boone, being involved in one of the innumerable law-suits which were about this time inflicted upon Kentucky, was deprived of his whole estate by an adverse decision. The indignation of the old hunter, at first, knew no bounds; but his tranquillity soon returned. He was, however, thoroughly disgusted with civilized society, and determined again, though gray with years, to find a home in the unbroken forest.

In 1798, having obtained a grant of two thousand acres of land from the Spanish authorities in upper Louisiana, now Missouri, he removed thither with his family, and settled at Charette. Here he devoted himself to his familiar pursuits of hunting and trapping, and in September, 1822, he died, being in his eighty-fifth year.

CHARLES XII. OF SWEDEN.

CHARLES XII. was born on the 27th June, 1682. He was the son of Charles XI., a harsh and despotic prince. From his earliest years, he glowed to imitate the heroic character of Alexander, and, in his eagerness to reign, caused himself to be declared king of Sweden at the age of fifteen. At his coronation, he boldly seized the crown from the hands of the archbishop of Upsal, and set it on his own head.

His youth seemed to invite the attacks of his neighbors, of Poland, Denmark and Russia; but Charles, unawed by the prospect of hostilities, and though scarcely eighteen, determined to assail his enemies, one after the other. He besieged Copenhagen, and, by his vigorous measures, so terrified the Danish monarch, that, in less than six weeks, he obliged him to sue for peace.

From humbled Denmark, he marched against the Russians; and though at the head of only eight thousand men, he attacked the enemy who were besieging Narva with one hundred thousand men. The conflict was dreadful; thirty thousand were slain, twenty thousand asked for quarter, and the rest were taken or destroyed; while the Swedes had only twelve hundred killed, and eight hundred wounded. From Narva, the victorious monarch advanced into Poland, defeated the Saxons who opposed his march, and obliged the Polish king, in suing for peace, to renounce his crown and acknowledge Stanislaus for his successor.

It was a disgraceful condition of the treaty made with Augustus that he should give up Reinhold Patkul, a Polish nobleman, to the Swedish king. This patriot had nobly defended the liberties of his country against its enemies, and to escape the consequences, when Poland had fallen, went to Russia, and entered into the service of the Czar. Peter sent him as ambassador to Poland, and Augustus delivered him up to Charles. He was taken to Stockholm, tried as a rebel and traitor, and broke on the wheel. Such was the justice, such the mercy, of the chivalrous Charles XII.!

Fixing his head quarters near Leipsic, with a victorious army of fifty thousand veteran Swedes, he now attracted the attention of all Europe. He received ambassadors from the principal powers, and even the Duke of Marlborough paid him a visit to induce him to join the allies against Louis XIV. But Charles had other views, which were to dethrone his rival, Peter of

Russia. Accordingly, after adjusting various matters, he proceeded to the north, with forty-three thousand men, in September, 1707.

In January, he defeated the Russians in Lithuania, and in June, 1708, met Peter on the banks of the Berezina. The Swedes crossed the river, and the Russians fled. Charles pursued them as far as Smolensk; but in September he began to experience the real difficulties of a Russian campaign. The country was desolate, the roads wretched, the winter approaching, and the army had hardly provisions for a fortnight. Charles, therefore, abandoned his plan of marching upon Moscow, and turned to the south towards the Ukraine, where Mazeppa, hetman or chief of the Cossacks, had agreed to join him against Peter.

Charles advanced towards the river Desna, an affluent of the Dnieper, which it joins near Kiew; but he missed his way among the extensive marshes which cover a great part of the country, and in which almost all his artillery and wagons were lost. Meantime, the Russians had dispersed Mazeppa's Cossacks, and Mazeppa himself came to join Charles as a fugitive with a small body of followers. Lowenhaupt, also, who was coming from Poland with fifteen thousand men, was defeated by Peter in person.

Charles thus found himself in the wilds of the Ukraine, hemmed in by the Russians, without provisions, and the winter setting in with unusual severity. His army, thinned by cold, hunger, fatigue and the sword, was now reduced to twenty-four thousand men. In this condition, he passed the winter in the Ukraine, his army subsisting chiefly by the exertions of Mazeppa. In the spring, with eighteen thousand Swedes and as many Cossacks, he laid siege to the town of Pultowa, where the Russians had collected large stores. During the siege, he was severely wounded in the foot; and soon after, Peter himself appeared to relieve Pultowa, at the head of seventy thousand men. Charles had now no choice but to risk a general battle, which was fought on the 8th of July, 1709, and ended in the total defeat of the Swedes.

At the close of the battle, Charles was placed on horseback, and, attended by about five hundred horse, who cut their way through more than ten Russian regiments, was conducted, for the space of a league, to the baggage of the Swedish army. In the flight, the king's horse was killed under him, and he was placed upon another. They selected a coach from the baggage, put Charles in it, and fled towards the Borysthenes with the utmost precipitation. He was silent for a time, but, at last, made some inquiries. Being informed of the fatal result of the battle, he said, cheerfully, "Come then, let us go to the Turks."

While he was making his escape, the Russians seized his artillery in the camp before Pultowa, his baggage and his military chest, in which they found six millions in specie, the spoils of Poland and Saxony. Nine thousand men, partly Swedes and partly Cossacks, were killed in the battle, and about six thousand were taken prisoners. There still remained about sixteen thousand men, including the Swedes, Poles and Cossacks, who fled towards the Borysthenes, under conduct of General Lowenhaupt.

He marched one way with his fugitive troops, and the king took another with some of his horse. The coach in which he rode broke down by the way, and they again set him on horseback. To complete his misfortune, he was separated from his troops and wandered all night in the woods; here, his courage being no longer able to support his exhausted spirits, the pain of his wound became more intolerable from fatigue, and his horse falling under him through excessive weariness, he lay some hours, at the foot of a tree, in danger of being surprised every moment by the conquerors, who were searching for him on every side.

At last, on the 10th July, at night, Charles reached the banks of the Borysthenes. Lowenhaupt had just arrived with the shattered remains of his army. It was with a mixture of joy and sorrow that the Swedes beheld their king, whom they had supposed dead. The victorious enemy was now approaching. The Swedes had neither a bridge to pass the river, nor time to make one, nor powder to defend themselves, nor provisions to support an army which had eaten nothing for two days. But more than all this, Charles was reduced to a state of extreme weakness by his wound, and was no longer himself. They carried him along like a sick person, in a state of insensibility.

Happily there was at hand a sorry calash, which by chance the Swedes had brought along with them; this they put on board a little boat, and the king and General Mazeppa embarked in another. The latter had saved several coffers of money; but the current being rapid, and a violent wind beginning to blow, the Cossacks threw more than three fourths of his treasure overboard to lighten the boat. Thus the king crossed the river, together with a small troop of horse, belonging to his guards, who succeeded in swimming the river. Every foot soldier who attempted to cross the stream was drowned.

Guided by the dead carcasses of the Swedes, that thickly strewed their path, a detachment of the Russian army came upon the fugitives. Some of the Swedes, reduced to despair, threw themselves into the river, while others took their own lives. The remainder capitulated, and were made slaves. Thousands of them were dispersed over Siberia, and never again returned to their country. In this barbarous region, rendered ingenious through necessity, they exercised trades and employments, of which they had not before the least idea.

All the distinctions which fortune had formerly established between them before, were now banished. The officer, who could not follow any trade, was obliged to cleave and carry wood for the soldier, now turned tailor, clothier, joiner, mason, or goldsmith, and who got a subsistence by his labors. Some of the officers became painters, and others architects; some of them taught the languages and mathematics. They even established some public schools, which in time became so useful and famous, that the citizens of Moscow sent their children thither for education.

The Swedish army, which had left Saxony in such a triumphant manner, was now no more. Three fourths had perished in battle, or by starvation, and the rest were slaves. Charles XII. had lost the fruit of nine years' labor, and almost one hundred battles. He had escaped in a wretched calash, attended by a small troop. These followed, some on foot, some on horseback, and others in wagons, through a desert, where neither huts, tents, men, beasts, nor roads were to be seen. Everything was wanting, even water itself.

It was now the beginning of July; the country lay in the forty-seventh degree of latitude; the dry sand of the desert rendered the heat of the sun the more insupportable; the horses fell by the way, and the men were ready to die with thirst. A brook of muddy water, which they found towards evening, was all they met with; they filled some bottles with this water, which saved the lives of the king's troops.

Triumphing over incredible difficulties, Charles and his little guard at last reached Benda, in the Turkish territory. He was hospitably received by the governor; and the sultan, Achmet III., gave orders that he should have entertainment and protection. He now attempted to induce the sultan to engage in his cause, but the Russian agents at the Turkish court produced an impression against him, and orders were sent to the governor of Benda, to compel the king to depart, and in case he refused, to bring him, living or dead, to Adrianople.

Little used to obey, Charles determined to resist. Having but two or three hundred men, he still disposed them in the best manner he could, and when attacked by the whole force of the Turkish army, he only yielded step by step. His house at last took fire, yet the king and his soldiers still resisted. When, involved in flames and smoke, he was about to abandon it, his spurs became entangled, and he fell and was taken prisoner. His eyelashes were singed by powder and his clothes were covered with blood. He was now removed to Demotica, near Adrianople. Here he spent two months in bed, feigning sickness, and employed in reading and writing.

Convinced, at last, that he could expect no assistance from the Porte, he set off, in disguise, with two officers. Accustomed to every deprivation, he pursued his journey on horseback, through Hungary and Germany, day and night, with such haste, that only one of his attendants was able to keep up with him. Exhausted and haggard, he arrived before Stralsund, about one o'clock, on the night of the 11th November, 1714.

Pretending to be a courier with important despatches from Turkey, he caused himself to be immediately introduced to the commandant, Count Dunker, who questioned him concerning the king, without recognising him till he began to speak, when he sprang, joyfully from his bed, and embraced the knees of his master. The report of Charles' arrival spread rapidly through the city. The houses were illuminated, and every demonstration of joy was exhibited.

A combined army of Danes, Saxons, Russians and Prussians now invested Stralsund. Charles performed miracles of bravery in its defence, but was obliged, at last, to surrender the fortress. Various events now took place, and negotiations were entered into for pacification with Russia. In the mean time, Charles had laid siege to Friedrichshall, in Norway. On the 3d of November, 1718, while in the trenches, and leaning against the parapet, examining the workmen, he was struck on the head by a cannon ball, and instantly killed. He was found dead in the same position, his hand on his sword; in his pocket were the portrait of Gustavus Adolphus, and a prayer-book. It is probable that the fatal ball was fired, not from the hostile fortress, but from the Swedish side; his adjutant, Siguier, has been accused as an accomplice in his murder.

The life of Charles XII. presents a series of marvellous events, yet his character inspires us with little respect or sympathy. He aspired only to be a military hero, and to reign by the power of his arms. He had the bravery, perseverance, and decision suited to the soldier, and that utter selfishness, and recklessness of human life and happiness, which are necessary ingredients in the character of a mere warrior. His cheerfulness in adversity, and his patient endurance of pain and privation, were counterbalanced by obstinacy, amounting almost to insanity. Charles had, indeed, the power of attaching friends strongly to his person; and there is something almost sublime in the utter disregard of comfort, pleasure, and even life, displayed by his soldiers and officers, in their care of his person, and their obedience to his commands. Yet, however elevating may be the sentiment of loyalty, we cannot feel that, in the present instance, it was bestowed upon a worthy object.

THE CID.

THIS celebrated hero of Spanish history has been for more than eight centuries the theme of eulogy and song, and doubtless his wonderful achievements and romantic fame have contributed to kindle an emulous flame in many a youthful bosom, and to stir up even a nation to the resistance of oppression. It is by no means improbable that many of the deeds of valor and patriotic devotion witnessed during the invasion of Spain by Napoleon's armies, had their source in the name and fame of the Cid. In one of the numerous ballads which recount his history, and which are among the popular poetry of Spain to this day, he is addressed in the following vigorous lines:—

"Mighty victor, never vanquished,
    Bulwark of our native land,
Shield of Spain, her boast and glory,
    Knight of the far-dreaded brand,
Venging scourge of Moors and traitors,
    Mighty thunderbolt of war,
Mirror bright of chivalry,
    Ruy, my Cid Campeador!"

This chivalrous knight was born at Burgos, in the year 1025. His name was Rodrigo, or Ruy Diaz, Count of Bivar. He was called the *Cid*, which means lord; and the name of *Campeador*, or champion without an equal, was appropriated as his peculiar title. At this period, the greater part of the Peninsula was in the hands of the Arabs or Moors, who had invaded them three centuries before. The few Goths who had remained unconquered among the mountains, maintained a constant warfare upon the infidels, and by the time of which we speak, they had recovered a large portion of the country lying in the northwestern quarter. This territory was divided into several petty kingdoms, or counties, the principal of which, at the time of our hero's birth, were united under Ferdinand I., the founder of the kingdom of Castile. The rest of the Peninsula, subject to the Arabs, was also divided into petty kingdoms.

The father of Rodrigo, Don Diego Lainez, was the representative of an ancient, wealthy, and noble race. When our hero was a mere stripling, his father was grossly insulted by the haughty and powerful Count of Gormaz, Don Lozano Gomez, who smote him in the face, in the very presence of the king and court. The dejection of the worthy hidalgo, who was very aged, and therefore incapable of taking personal vengeance for his wrong, is thus strongly depicted in one of the ballads:—

> "Sleep was banished from his eyelids;
>   Not a mouthful could he taste;
> There he sat with downcast visage,—
>   Direly had he been disgraced.
>
> Never stirred he from his chamber;
>   With no friends would he converse,
> Lest the breath of his dishonor
>   Should pollute them with its curse."

When young Rodrigo, the son, was informed of the indignity offered to his father, he was greatly incensed, and determined to avenge it. He accordingly took down an old sword, which had been the instrument of mighty deeds in the hands of his ancestors, and, mounting a horse, proceeded to challenge the haughty Count Gomez, in the following terms:—

> "How durst thou to smite my father?
>   Craven caitiff! know that none
> Unto him shall do dishonor,
>   While I live, save God alone.
>
> For this wrong, I must have vengeance,—
>   Traitor, here I thee defy!
> With thy blood alone my sire
>   Can wash out his infamy!"

The count despised his youth, and refused his challenge; but the boy set bravely upon him, and, after a fierce conflict, was victorious. He bore the bleeding head of his antagonist to his father, who greeted him with rapture.

His fame was soon spread abroad, and he was reckoned among the bravest squires of the time.

But now there appeared before king Ferdinand and the court of Burgos the lovely Ximena, daughter of the Count Gomez, demanding vengeance of the sovereign for the death of her father. She fell on her knees at the king's feet, crying for justice.

> "Justice, king! I sue for justice—
>   Vengeance on a traitorous knight;
> Grant it me! so shall thy children
>   Thrive, and prove thy soul's delight."

When she had spoken these words, her eye fell on Rodrigo, who stood among the attendant nobles, and she exclaimed,—

> "Thou hast slain the best and bravest
>   That e'er set a lance in rest,
> Of our holy faith the bulwark,—
>   Terror of each Paynim breast.
>
> Traitorous murderer, slay me also!
>   Though a woman, slaughter me!
> Spare not! I'm Ximena Gomez,
>   Thine eternal enemy!
>
> Here's my heart,—smite, I beseech thee!
>   Smite! and fatal be thy blow!
> Death is all I ask, thou caitiff,—
>   Grant this boon unto thy foe."

Not a word, however, did Rodrigo reply, but, seizing the bridle of his steed, he vaulted into the saddle, and rode slowly away. Ximena turned to the crowd of nobles, and seeing that none prepared to follow him and take up her cause, she cried aloud, "Vengeance, sirs, I pray you vengeance!" A second time did the damsel disturb the king, when at a banquet, with her cries for justice. She had now a fresh complaint.

"Every day at early morning,
    To despite me more, I wist,
He who slew my sire doth ride by,
    With a falcon on his fist.

At my tender dove he flies it;
    Many of them hath it slain.
See, their blood hath dyed my garments,
    With full many a crimson stain."

Rodrigo, however, was not punished, and the king suspected that this conduct of the young count was only typical of his purpose to hawk at the lady himself, and make her the captive of love. He was therefore left to pursue his career; and he soon performed an achievement which greatly increased his fame. Five Moorish chiefs or kings, and their attendants, had made a foray into the Castilian territories, and, being unresisted, were bearing off immense booty and many captives. Rodrigo, though still a youth under twenty, mounted his horse, Babieca, as famous in his story as is Bucephalus in that of Alexander, hastily gathered a host of armed men, and fell suddenly upon the Moors, among the mountains of Oca. He routed them with great slaughter, captured the five kings, and recovered all that they had taken.

The spoil he divided among his followers, but reserved the kings for his own share, and carried them home to his castle of Bivar, to present them, as proofs of his prowess, to his mother. With his characteristic generosity, which was conspicuous even at this early age, he then set them at liberty, on their agreeing to pay him tribute; and they departed to their respective territories, lauding his valor and magnanimity.

The fame of this exploit soon spread far and wide, through the land, and as martial valor in those chivalrous times was the surest passport to ladies' favor, it must have had its due effect on Ximena's mind, and will, in a great measure, account for the entire change in her sentiments towards the youth, which she manifested on another visit to Burgos. Falling on her knees before the king, she spoke thus:—

"I am daughter of Don Gomez,
    Count of Gormaz was he hight;
Him Rodrigo by his valor
    Did o'erthrow in mortal fight.

King! I come to crave a favor—
    This the boon for which I pray,
That thou give me this Rodrigo
    For my wedded lord this day.

Grant this precious boon, I pray thee;
    'Tis a duty thou dost owe;
For the great God hath commanded
    That we should forgive a foe."

There is a touch of nature in all this, that is quite amusing: while the lady's anger burns, she cries for justice; when love has taken possession of her heart, she appeals to religion to enforce her wishes. "Now I see," said the king, "how true it is, what I have often heard, that the will of woman is wild and strange. Hitherto this damsel hath sought deadly vengeance on the youth, and now she would have him to husband. Howbeit, with right good will I will grant what she desireth."

He sent at once for Rodrigo, who, with a train of three hundred young nobles, his friends and kinsmen, all arrayed in new armor and robes of brilliant color, obeyed with all speed the royal summons. The king rode forth to meet him, "for right well did he love Rodrigo," and opened the matter to him, promising him great honors and much land if he would make Ximena his bride. Rodrigo, who desired nothing better, and who doubtless had hoped for this issue, at once acquiesced.

"King and lord! right well it pleaseth
    Me thy wishes to fulfil:
In this thing, as in all others,
    I obey thy sovereign will."

The young pair then plighted their troth in presence of the king, and in pledge thereof gave him their hands. He kept his promise, and gave Rodrigo

Valduerna, Saldana, Belforado, and San Pedro de Cardena, for a marriage portion.

The wedding was attended by vast pomp and great festivities. Rodrigo, sumptuously attired, went with a long procession to the church. After a while, Ximena came, with a veil over her head and her hair dressed in large plaits, hanging over her ears. She wore an embroidered gown of fine London cloth, and a close-fitting spencer. She walked on high-heeled clogs of red leather. A necklace of eight medals or plates of gold, with a small pendent image of St. Michael, which together were "worth a city," encircled her white neck.

The happy pair met, seized each other's hands, and embraced. Then said Rodrigo, with great emotion, as he gazed on his bride,—

> "I did slay thy sire, Ximena,
>   But, God wot, not traitorously;
> 'Twas in open fight I slew him:
>   Sorely had he wronged me.
>
> A man I slew,—a man I give thee,—
>   Here I stand thy will to bide!
> Thou, in place of a dead father,
>   Hast a husband at thy side."
>
> All approved well his prudence,
>   And extolled him with zeal;
> Thus they celebrate the nuptials
>   Of Rodrigo of Castile.

We cannot attend this renowned hero through his long and brilliant career. We must be content to say, that on all occasions he displayed every noble and heroic quality. His life was an almost perpetual strife with the Moors, whom he defeated in many combats. Having collected a considerable force, on one occasion, he penetrated to the southeastern extremity of Arragon, and established himself in a strong castle, still called the Rock of the Cid. He afterwards pushed his victories to the borders of the Mediterranean, and laid siege to the rich and powerful Moorish city of Valencia, which he captured. Here he established his kingdom, and continued to reign till his death, about the year 1099, at the age of seventy-five.

While the Cid was living, his reputation was sufficient to keep the Moors in awe; but when he was dead, their courage revived, and they boldly attacked the Spaniards, even in Valencia, the city where his remains were laid. The Spaniards went forth to meet them; and behold, a warrior, with the well known dress of the Cid, but with the aspect of death, was at their head. The Moors recognised his features, and they fled in superstitious horror, fancying that a miracle had been performed in behalf of the Spaniards. The truth was, however, that the latter had taken him from the tomb, set him on his warhorse, and thus, even after his death, he achieved a victory over his foes. This incident sufficiently attests the wonderful power which the Cid's name exerted, as well over his countrymen as their enemies.

The Spaniards have an immense number of ballads and romances, founded upon the life of this wonderful hero. They all depict him as a noble and high-minded chief, without fear and without reproach, the very *beau ideal* of a knight of the olden time. Some of these ballads are finely rendered into English by Mr. Lockhart, and they have been published in a style of unsurpassed beauty and splendor.

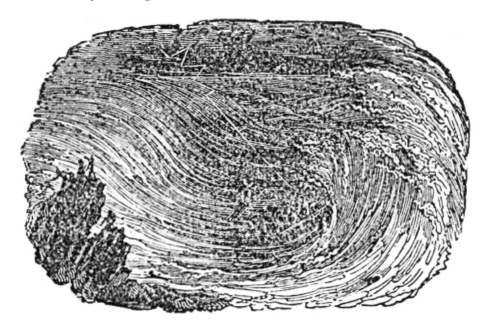

ROBIN HOOD.

IT may seem strange that an outlaw, a thief and a robber, should be a favorite theme of song and of story, and continue to command the respect of mankind for centuries after the period of his existence: yet such is the fact in respect to the subject of the present sketch. He was born at Lockslay, near Nottingham, about the year 1150, and flourished during the time of Richard I. of England.

Nearly a century before this, William of Normandy had conquered England, and established the Norman sway in that realm. The great estates passed into the hands of French chiefs and barons; and while nearly all the higher ranks of society, at the period of which we speak, were French, the other classes consisted of native Saxons. Between these distinct races and orders, a natural jealousy existed, which was in no small degree cherished by the laws and policy of the government, which tended at once to oppress the people and extend the privileges of the nobles.

The game laws, which punished those who should kill game in the royal forests, by putting out the eyes, and other mutilations, excited the deepest indignation. The yeomanry of the country were, at this time, universally trained in the use of the bow, and, notwithstanding the severity of the laws, those living around the king's parks frequently shot the game. These persons were so numerous, that they finally associated together in considerable bands, for mutual protection. Many of them devoted themselves entirely to robbing the parks, and became not only skilful in the use of the bow, but familiar with the recesses and hiding-places of the forests, and expert in every device, either for plunder, concealment, or escape.

Of all the leaders of these several bands, Robin Hood became the most famous; for he was not only bold and skilful in forest craft, but he appears to have been guided by noble and patriotic sentiments. According to one of the many ballads which set forth his adventures, he displayed his courage and dexterity at a very early age.

> "Robin Hood would into Nottingham go,
>   When the summer days were fine,

And there he saw fifteen foresters bold,
　　A drinking good ale and wine.

'What news? what news?' said bold Robin Hood,
　　'The news I fain would know;
If our king hath ordered a shooting match,
　　I am ready with my bow.'"

The foresters stared at him, and said, "We hold it a scorn for one so young, presuming to bear a bow, who is not able to draw a string." "I'll hold you twenty marks," said Robin, "that I will hit a mark a hundred rods off, and cause a hart to die." "We hold you twenty marks, by our lady's leave," replied the foresters, "that you neither hit the mark at that distance, nor kill a hart."

"Then Robin Hood bent his noble bow,
　　And a broad arrow he let fly;
He hit the mark a hundred rod,
　　And he caused a hart to die.

The hart did skip, and the hart did leap,
　　And the hart lay on the ground;
'The wager is mine,' said bold Robin Hood,
　　'An' 'twere for a thousand pounds.'"

The foresters laughed, and taunted the proud archer, and also refused to pay the twenty marks, and advised him to be gone, lest blows should follow. He picked up his arrows and his bow, and was observed to smile as he retired from these discourteous churls. When at some distance, he paused,—

"Then Robin he bent his noble bow,
　　And broad arrows he let flye;
Till fourteen of these fifteen foresters
　　Upon the ground did lye."

Sherwood forest, near Nottingham, was the chief theatre of Robin Hood's achievements. At one time he had no less than a hundred archers at his command, a gallant woodsman, by the name of Little John, being his particular friend and favorite. There was also among the merry crew, a mock friar, by the name of Tuck, who appears to have been full of mirth and humor.

Robin's orders to his men were, always to spare the common people; to aid and assist the weak; to be scrupulous never to injure or insult a woman; to be the friend of the poor, the timid, and the oppressed; but to plunder fat bishops, lazy friars, purse-proud squires, and haughty barons. His system was, to take from the rich, and give to the poor; and while he ever observed this rule himself, he enforced it rigorously among all his followers. His history is full of details in which he illustrates these principles.

Robin became so notorious at last, that a price was offered for his apprehension, and several attempts were made to deliver him up; but his courage and dexterity, or his faithful friends, always saved him. One of the old ballads relates an adventure with a stout tinker, who, among others, sought to capture the redoubted outlaw. According to this story, Robin met him in the greenwood, and bade him good morrow; adding, "pray where live ye, and what is your trade? I hear there are sad news stirring." "Aye, indeed!" answered the other; "I am a tinker, and live at Banbury, and the news of which you speak have not reached me."

> "'As for the news,' quoth Robin Hood,
>   'It is but, as I hear,
> Two tinkers were set in the stocks,
>   For drinking ale and beer.'
>
> 'If that be all,' the tinker said,
>   'As I may say to you,
> Your tidings are not worth a groat,
>   So be they were all true.'"

"Well," said Robin, "I love ale and beer when they are good, with all my heart, and so the fault of thy brethren is small: but I have told all my news; now tell me thine."

> "'All the news I have,' the tinker said,
>   'And they are news for good;
> It is to seek the bold outlaw,
>   Whom men call Robin Hood.

> I have a warrant from the king,
>   To take him where I can,
> And if you can tell me where he dwells,
>   I will make of you a man.'"

"That I can readily do," replied the outlaw; "let me look at the warrant." "Nay, nay," said the tinker, "I'll trust that with no man." "Well," answered the other, "be it as you please; come with me, and I'll show you Robin Hood." To accomplish this, Robin took him to an inn, where the ale and wine were so good and plentiful, and the tinker so thirsty, that he drank till he fell asleep; and when he awoke, he found that the outlaw had not only left him to pay the reckoning, which was beyond his means, but had stolen the king's warrant. "Where is my friend?" exclaimed the tinker, starting up. "Your friend?" said mine host; "why, men call him Robin Hood, and he meant you evil when he met with you." The tinker left his working-bag and hammer as a pledge for the reckoning, and, snatching up his crab-tree club, sallied out after Robin. "You'll find him killing the king's deer, I'll be sworn," shouted the landlord; and, accordingly, among the deer he found him. "What knave art thou," said the outlaw, "that dare come so near the king of Sherwood?"

> "'No knave, no knave,' the tinker said,
>   'And that you soon shall know;
> Which of us have done most wrong,
>   My crab-tree staff shall show.'
>
> Then Robin drew his gallant blade,
>   Made of the trusty steel,
> But the tinker he laid on so fast,
>   That he made Robin reel."

This raised the outlaw's wrath, and he exerted his skill and courage so well, that the tinker more than once thought of flight; but the man of Banbury was stubborn stuff, and at last drove Robin to ask a favor.

> "'A boon, a boon,' Robin he cries,
>   'If thou wilt grant it me;'

'Before I'll do 't,' the tinker said,
　　'I'll hang thee on a tree.'

But the tinker looking him about,
　　Robin his horn did blow;
Then unto him came Little John,
　　And brave Will Scarlet too."

"Now what is the matter, master," said Little John, "that you sit thus by the way-side?" "You may ask the tinker there," said Robin; "he hath paid me soundly." "I must have a bout with him, then," said the other, "and see if he can do as much for me." "Hold, hold," cried Robin; "the tinker's a jovial fellow, and a stout."

"'In manhood he's a mettled man,
　　And a metal man by trade;
Never thought I that any man
　　Should have made me so afraid.

And if he will be one of us,
　　We will take all one fare;
Of gold and good, whate'er we get,
　　The tinker he shall share.'"

The tinker was not a man of many words; he nodded assent, and added another bold forester to the ranks of the outlaw.

Robin and his friends were so sharply hunted by the sheriff of Nottinghamshire, that they deemed it prudent to retire to the forests of Barnesdale, where they gaily pursued their calling. Their interference in church matters, in various ways, gave offence to his reverence, the Bishop of Hereford, who declared that measures should be taken to repress the insolence of the outlaw, and he promised to look strictly into the matter the first time he chanced to be near Barnesdale. It was on a sunny morning that Robin heard of the bishop's approach, "with all his company," and his joy was excessive.

"'Go, kill me a fat buck,' said bold Robin Hood,
　　'Go slay me a fair fat deer;

The Bishop of Hereford dines with me to-day,
    And he shall pay well for his cheer.'"

Accordingly, the deer was killed and skinned, and laid to the fire, and, with six of his men habited like shepherds, Robin was pacing round and round, as the wooden spit with its savory load revolved, when up came the Bishop of Hereford, who halted, and exclaimed, "What is all this, my masters? For whom do you make such a feast, and of the king's venison? Verily, I must look into this." "We are shepherds, simple shepherds, sir," replied the outlaw meekly. "We keep sheep the whole year round, and as this is our holiday, we thought there was no harm in holding it on one of the king's deer, of which there are plenty." "You are fine fellows," said the bishop, "mighty fine fellows; but the king shall know of your doings; so quit your roast, for to him you shall go, and that quickly."

"'O pardon, pardon,' cried bold Robin Hood,
    'O pardon of thee I pray;
O it ill becomes a holy bishop's coat,
    For to take men's lives away.'

'No pardon, no pardon,' the bishop he said,
    'No pardon to thee I owe;
Therefore make haste, for I swear by St. Paul
    Before the king you shall go.'"

Upon this, the outlaw sprung back against a tree, and setting his horn to his mouth, made in a moment all the wood to ring. It was answered, as usual, by the sudden appearance of threescore and ten of his comrades, who, with Little John at their head, overpowered the bishop's guard, and then inquired of Robin what was the matter that he blew a blast so sharp and startling.

"'O here is the Bishop of Hereford,
    And no pardon shall we have;'
'Ho, cut off his head, then,' quoth Little John,
    'And I'll go make him a grave.'

'O pardon, pardon,' then cried the bishop,
    'O pardon of thee I pray;

> O had I known that you were so near,
> > I'd have gone some other way.'"

Now Robin had no pleasure in shedding blood, but he loved to enjoy the terrors of those whom he captured: and to keep them in suspense, while he feasted them on the best, was a favorite practice of his. It was in this spirit that he now spoke:

> "'No pardon, no pardon,' said bold Robin Hood,
> > 'No pardon to thee I owe;
> Therefore make haste, for I swear by my bow
> > That to Barnesdale with me you go.'

> Then Robin he took the bishop by the hand,
> > And led him to merry Barnesdale,
> And he supped that night in the clear moonlight,
> > On the good red wine and ale."

How this was to end, the bishop seems to have had a guess. The parody which the outlaw made on his threats of carrying him to the king, showed that he was in a pleasant mood; and the venison collops, and the wine and ale, all evinced a tendency to mercy; of which, as it was now late, he took advantage. "I wish, mine host," said the bishop, with a sort of grave good-nature, "that you would call a reckoning; it is growing late, and I begin to fear that the cost of such an entertainment will be high." Here Little John interposed, for Robin affected great ignorance in domestic matters, leaving the task of fleecing his guests to his expert dependents. "Lend me your purse, master," said his scrupulous deputy to the bishop, "and I'll tell you all by-and-by."

> "Then Little John took the bishop's cloak,
> > And spread it upon the ground,
> And out of the bishop's portmanteau
> > He told three hundred pound.

> 'Here's gold enough, master,' said Little John,
> > "Tis a comely thing for to see;
> It puts me in charity with the good bishop,

Though he heartily loveth not me.'

Robin Hood took the bishop by the hand,
    And causing the music to play,
He made the good bishop to dance in his boots,
    And glad he could so get away."

If we may put trust in ballad and song, the loss of the three hundred pounds dwelt on the bishop's mind, and at the head of a fair company he went in quest of his entertainer. He had well nigh taken Robin by surprise, for he was upon him before he was aware; but the outlaw escaped into an old woman's house, to whom he called, "Save my life; I am Robin Hood, and here comes the bishop, to take me and hang me." "Aye, that I will," said the old woman, "and not the less willingly that you gave me hose and shoon, when I greatly needed them." It was thus that the robber always found friends among the poor, for he was uniformly their protector and benefactor.

According to one of the ballads, king Edward had become deeply incensed against Robin, and went to Nottingham to bring him to justice. But in vain did he seek to get a sight of him; at last, however, dressed in the disguise of a monk, he met him, and dined with him and his merry men in the forest. After a time, the king was recognised by the outlaw, who bent his knee in homage, and, upon an assurance of safety, went with him to Nottingham, where he was nobly entertained, in the midst of the court. He soon, however, became sick of this kind of life, and joyfully returned to the greenwood.

But there is no safeguard against the approach of death. Time and toil began to do with Robin Hood all that they do with lesser spirits. One morning he had tried his shafts, and found that they neither flew so far as they were wont, nor with their usual accuracy of aim; and he thus addressed Little John, the most faithful of his companions:—

    "'I am not able to shoot a shot more,
        Mine arrows refuse to flee;
    But I have a cousin lives down below,
        Who, please God, will bleed me.'"

Now this cousin was prioress of Kirkley Nunnery, in Yorkshire, and seems to have had no good-will to Robin, whom she doubtless regarded as a godless and graceless person, who plundered church and churchmen, and set laws, both sacred and profane, at defiance.

> "Now Robin is to fair Kirkley gone,
>   He knocked low at the ring;
> And none came there save his cousin dear,
>   To let bold Robin in.
>
> 'Thrice welcome now, cousin Robin,' she said;
>   'Come drink some wine with me;'
> 'No, cousin, I'll neither eat nor drink
>   Till I blooded am by thee.'"

She took him to a lonely room, and bled him, says the ballad, till one drop more refused to run: then she locked him in the place, with the vein unbound, and left him to die. This was in the morning; and the day was near the close, when Robin, thinking the prioress was long in returning, tried to rise, but was unable, and, bethinking him of his bugle when it was too late, snatched it up, and blew three blasts. "My master must be very ill," said Little John, "for he blows wearily," and, hurrying to the nunnery, was refused admittance; but, "breaking locks two or three," he found Robin all but dead, and, falling on his knee, begged as a boon to be allowed to "burn Kirkley Hall, with all its nunnery." "Nay, nay," replied Robin, "I never hurt a woman in all my life, nor yet a man in woman's company. As it has been during my life, so shall it be at my end."

> "'But give me my bent bow in my hand,
>   A broad arrow I'll let flee,
> And where this shaft doth chance to fall,
>   There shall my grave digged be.
>
> And lay my bent bow by my side,
>   Which was my music sweet;
> And cover my grave with sod so green,
>   As is both right and meet.

And let me have breadth and length enough,
    By the side of yon green wood,
That men may say, when they look on it,
    Here lies bold Robin Hood.'"

Having given these directions, he died, and was buried as he directed, under some fine trees near Kirkley, and a stone with an inscription was laid on the grave. Little John, it is said, survived only to see his master buried. His burial-place is claimed by Scotland as well as by England; but tradition inclines to the grave in the church-yard of Hathersage.

The bond of union which had held his men so long together, was now broken; some made their peace with the government, others fled to foreign parts, and nothing remained of Robin Hood but a name which is to be found in history, in the drama, in ballads, in songs, in sayings, and in proverbs.

PAUL JONES.

THIS hero of the American Revolution was born on the 6th of July, 1747, on the estate of Arbigland, in the parish of Kirkbean, Scotland. His father was a gardener, whose name was Paul, but the son assumed that of Jones, after his settlement in America. The birthplace of young Paul was a bold promontory, jutting into the sea, and was well calculated to excite a love of the briny element, for which he soon displayed a decided predilection.

At the age of twelve, he was bound apprentice to a merchant of Whitehaven, in the American trade. He soon after went to sea, in a vessel bound for Virginia. While in port, he spent his time on shore with his brother William, who was a respectable planter in the colony. He devoted himself to the study of navigation and other subjects connected with the profession he had chosen. These he pursued with great steadiness, displaying those habits of industrious application, which raised him to the distinguished place he afterwards attained. His good conduct secured him the respect of his employers, and he rose rapidly in his profession.

At the age of nineteen, he had become the chief mate of the Two Friends, a slave ship, belonging to Jamaica. At this period, the traffic in slaves was exceedingly profitable, and was followed without scruple or reproach by the most respectable merchants of Bristol and Liverpool. But young Paul had pursued this business for only a short time, when he became so shocked and sickened at the misery which it inflicted upon the negroes, that he left it forever in disgust.

In 1768, he sailed from Jamaica for Scotland, as a passenger. Both the master and mate dying of fever on the voyage, he assumed the command, and arrived safely at port. Gratified by his conduct, the owners placed him on board the brig John, as master and supercargo, and despatched him to the West Indies. He made a second voyage in the same vessel, during which he inflicted punishment on the carpenter, named Maxwell, for mutinous conduct. As Maxwell died of fever, soon after, Paul was charged, by persons who envied his rising reputation, with having caused his death by excessive punishment. This has been since abundantly disproved. Paul continued some time in the West India trade, but in 1773, he went to Virginia to arrange the affairs of his brother William, who had died without children, leaving no will. His brother was reported to have left a large estate; but as Paul was, soon after, in a state of penury, it is probable that this was a mistake. He now devoted himself to agriculture, but his planting operations do not seem to have prospered.

The American Revolution soon broke out, and considering himself a settled resident of the country, he determined to take her part in the bloody struggle which was about to follow. Impelled by a noble enthusiasm for the cause of liberty, a spirit of adventure, and a chivalrous thirst for glory, he offered his services to Congress, which were accepted, and he was commissioned as a lieutenant in the navy, in December, 1775. At this time, he bore the name of Jones, which he had perhaps assumed to conceal his conduct from his family, who might be pained to know that one of their name had taken part against England.

Jones was appointed first lieutenant of the Alfred, a flag-ship, and when the commander-in-chief came on board, he hoisted the American flag, with his own hands, being the first time it was ever displayed. At that time, the flag is said to have borne a device, representing a pine tree, with a rattlesnake coiled at the root, as if about to strike. The standard of the stars and stripes was not adopted till nearly two years later.

At this period, our hero was in the twenty-ninth year of his age. His figure was light, graceful and active, yet his health was good, his constitution vigorous, and he was capable of great endurance. There was in his countenance an expression of mingled sternness and melancholy, and his bearing was decidedly officer-like.

The first American squadron fitted out during the revolution, sailed in 1776. Jones was on board the Alfred in this expedition, but subsequently received the command of the sloop of war Providence. In this he cruised along the coast, meeting with a variety of adventures, in which he displayed admirable skill and coolness of conduct. On one occasion, he was chased by the British frigate Milford, off the Isle of Sable. Finding his vessel the faster of the two, he hovered near the frigate, yet beyond the reach of her shot. She, however, continued to pour forth her broadsides. This excited the contempt of Jones, and, with a humor peculiar to himself, he ordered the blustering battery of the frigate to be answered by a single shot from the musket of a marine.

Jones pursued his career with great industry and success. He seemed to glide over the seas like a hawk, passing rapidly from point to point, and pouncing upon such prey as he could master. Some of his feats resemble the prodigies of the days of chivalry. He seemed to court adventure and to sport with danger, yet a cool discretion presided over his conduct. In the year 1776, he captured no less than sixteen prizes in the space of six weeks.

Notwithstanding these signal services, Jones was superseded in the command of the Alfred, probably through the mean jealousy of Commodore Hopkins. There is, perhaps, no higher proof of elevation of character than is furnished by a calm and dignified endurance of injustice and ingratitude. This evidence was afforded by Jones, who, while he remonstrated against the injury that was done him, steadily adhered to the cause he had espoused, and exerted his abilities to the utmost to bear it forward with success. His letters of this period are full of enlightened views on the subject of naval affairs, and of hearty zeal in the cause of liberty. They show that his mind was far above mere personal considerations, and that even with statesman-like sagacity he looked forward to the establishment of a naval power in the United States, suited to the exigencies of the country.

The time for a recognition of his services speedily arrived. In 1777, he received orders from Congress to proceed in the French merchant ship Amphitrite, with officers and seamen, to take command of a heavy ship, to be provided for him by the American commissioners, Franklin, Dean and Lee, on his arrival in Europe. These he met at Paris, and arrangements were made by which he received the command of the Ranger, in which he sailed from Brest, on the 10th of April, 1778.

An insight into the views of Jones, at this period, as well as his general character, may be gathered from the following extract from one of his letters:—"I have in contemplation several enterprises of some importance. When an enemy thinks a design against him improbable, he can always be surprised and attacked with advantage. It is true, I must run great risk, but no gallant action was ever performed without danger. Therefore, though I cannot ensure success, I will endeavor to deserve it."

In fulfilment of these views, he set sail, and in four days after, captured and burnt a brigantine loaded with flaxseed, near Cape Clear. On the 17th, he took a ship bound for Dublin, which he manned and ordered to Brest. On the 19th, he took and sunk a schooner; on the 20th, a sloop; and soon after, made a daring, but unsuccessful attempt to capture, by surprise, the English sloop of war Drake, of twenty guns, lying in the loch of Belfast.

On the 22d, he determined to attack Whitehaven, with which he was of course well acquainted. The number of ships lying here amounted to two hundred and fifty, and were protected by two batteries, mounting thirty pieces of artillery. The attack was made in the dead of night, and while the unsuspecting inhabitants lay wrapped in repose. Roused to this daring enterprise by the fires, massacres, and ravages inflicted by the British forces upon the unprotected inhabitants of the American coast, and determined to check them by one signal and fearful act of retaliation, Jones pursued his measures with a stern and daring hand.

He proceeded, in the first place, to secure the forts, which were scaled, the soldiers made prisoners, and the guns spiked. He now despatched the greater portion of his men to set fire to the shipping, while he proceeded with a single follower to another fort, the guns of which he spiked. On returning to the ships, he found, to his mortification, that his orders had not been obeyed, from a reluctance, on the part of the seamen, to perform the task assigned them. One ship only was destroyed, which was set on fire by Jones himself.

Greatly disappointed at the partial failure of his scheme, Jones proceeded to the Scottish shore, for the purpose of carrying off the person of the Earl of Selkirk, whose gardener his father had been. The earl, however, was absent, and this part of the design failed. His men, however, proceeded to the earl's residence, and carried off his plate. Lady Selkirk was present, but she was treated with respect. Jones took no part in this enterprise, and only consented to it upon the urgent demands of his crew.

By this time, the people on both sides of the Irish channel were thoroughly roused by the daring proceedings of the Ranger. On the morning of the 24th April, Jones was hovering near Belfast, and the Drake worked out of the bay, to meet him. She had on board a large number of volunteers, making her crew amount to one hundred and sixty men. Alarm smokes were now seen rising on both sides of the channel, and several vessels loaded with people, curious to witness the coming engagement, were upon the water. As evening was approaching, however, they prudently put back.

Soon after, the two vessels met, and Jones poured in his first broadside. This was returned with energy, and a fearful conflict ensued. Running broadside and broadside, the most deadly fire was kept up. At last, after the struggle had been sustained at close quarters for more than an hour, the captain of the Drake was shot through the head, and his crew called for quarter. The loss of the Drake, in killed and wounded, was forty-two, while the Ranger had one seaman killed and seven wounded.

This victory was the more remarkable as the Drake carried twenty guns, and the Ranger but eighteen, and moreover belonged to a regular navy; while the Ranger was fitted up with little experience and under few advantages. Jones now set sail with his prize, and both vessels arrived safely at Brest, on the 8th May. Immediately after, Jones despatched a very romantic epistle to Lady Selkirk, apologizing for the violence that had been committed at the estate of the earl, and explaining the motives of his conduct. He promised to return the plate, which he afterwards accomplished with infinite difficulty.

It eventually reached England, though some years after, in the same condition in which it had been taken; even the tea leaves in the tea-pot remaining as they were found. An acknowledgment of its receipt, by the earl, was sent to Jones, with a recognition of the courteous behavior of the Ranger's crew when they landed on Saint Mary's Isle.

Being now at Brest with two hundred prisoners of war, Jones became involved in a variety of troubles, for want of means to support them, pay his crew and refit his ship. After many delays and vexations, he sailed from the road of Saint Croix, August 14, 1779, with a squadron of seven sail, designing to annoy the coasts of England and Scotland. The principal occurrence of this cruise was the capture of the British ship of war Serapis, after a bloody and desperate engagement, off Flamborough Head, September 23, 1779. The Serapis was a vessel much superior in force to Jones' vessel, the Bon Homme Richard, which sunk not long after the termination of the engagement.

The sensation produced by this battle was unexampled, and raised the fame of Jones to its height. In a letter to him, Franklin says, "For some days after the arrival of your express, scarce anything was talked of at Paris and Versailles but your cool conduct and persevering bravery during that terrible conflict. You may believe that the impression on my mind was not less than on that of the others. But I do not choose to say, in a letter to yourself, all I think on such an occasion."

His reception at Paris, whither he went on the invitation of Franklin, was of the most flattering kind. He was everywhere caressed; the king presented him with a gold sword, and requested permission of Congress to invest him with the military order of merit—an honor never conferred on any one before, who had not borne arms under the commission of France.

In 1781, Jones sailed for the United States, and arrived in Philadelphia, February 18, of that year, after a variety of escapes and encounters, where he underwent a sort of examination before the board of admiralty, which resulted greatly to his honor. The board gave it as their opinion, "that the conduct of Paul Jones merits particular attention, and some distinguished mark of approbation from Congress." That body accordingly passed a resolution highly complimentary to his "zeal, prudence, and intrepidity." General Washington wrote him a letter of congratulation, and he was afterwards voted a gold medal by Congress.

From Philadelphia, he went to Portsmouth, New Hampshire, to superintend the building of a ship of war, and, while there, drew up some admirable observations on the subject of the American navy. By permission of Congress, he subsequently went on board the French fleet, where he remained until the peace, which put a period to his naval career in the service of the United States. He then went to Paris as agent for prize money, and while there, joined in a plan to establish a fur-trade between the north-west coast of America and China, in conjunction with a kindred spirit, the celebrated John Ledyard.

In Paris he continued to be treated with the greatest distinction. He afterwards was invited into the Russian service, with the rank of rear-admiral, where he was disappointed in not receiving the command of the fleet acting against the Turks in the Black Sea. He condemned the conduct of the prince of Nassau, the admiral; became restless and impatient; was intrigued against at court, and calumniated by his enemies; and had permission from the empress Catherine to retire from the service with a pension, which, however, was never paid. He returned to Paris, where he gradually sunk into poverty, neglect and ill health, and finally died of dropsy, July 18, 1792.

MASANIELLO.

THOMASO ANIELLO, called by corruption Masaniello, was born at Amalfi, in Italy, about the year 1622. He established himself at Naples, where he obtained a living by catching and vending fish. At this period, Naples belonged to Spain, and the Duke D'Arcos governed it as viceroy. The city was suffering under many political evils. Its treasures went to Spain, and its youth were sent to fill up the ranks of the Spanish army; and both were wasted in ruinous wars, for the ambition and selfish views of a distant court.

In addition to all this, the people were oppressed with taxes, and outraged by the wanton tyranny of the officers of a foreign power. At last, in the year 1647, the Duke D'Arcos, in order to defray the expenses of a war against France, laid a tax on fruit and vegetables, the common articles of food of the Neapolitan people. This edict occasioned the greatest ferment, especially among the poorer inhabitants. Masaniello, who was now about twenty-five years of age, and a great favorite at the market-place, on account of his natural quickness and humor, denounced the tax in no measured terms. He seems to have perceived and felt the despotism that oppressed the people, and was, moreover, incited to opposition by an event which touched him personally.

His wife was one day arrested, as she was entering the city, attempting to smuggle a small quantity of flour,—an article which bore a heavy tax. She was accordingly, seized and imprisoned; nor could Masaniello obtain her release, but upon paying a considerable sum. Thus the fire which was soon to burst forth into conflagration was already kindling in his soul. Opportunity was only wanting, and this was soon offered.

Masaniello was at the head of a troop of young men who were preparing for the great festival of our Lady of the Carmel, by exhibiting sham combats, and a mock attack on a wooden castle. On the 7th July, 1647, he and his juvenile troops were standing in the market-place, where, in consequence of the obnoxious tax, but few countrymen had come with the produce of their gardens. The people looked sullen and dissatisfied. A dispute arose between a countryman and a customer who had bought some figs, as to which of the two was to bear the burden of the tax.

The *eletto*, a municipal magistrate, acting as provost of the trade, being appealed to, decided against the countryman; upon which the latter, in a rage, upset the basket of figs upon the pavement. A crowd soon collected round the man, who was cursing the tax and the tax-gatherer. Masaniello ran to the spot, crying out, "No taxes, no more taxes!" The cry was caught and repeated by a thousand voices. The *eletto* tried to speak to the multitude, but Masaniello threw a bunch of figs in his face; the rest of the people fell upon him, and he and his attendants escaped with difficulty.

Masaniello then addressed the people round him in a speech of coarse, hot, fiery eloquence; he described their common grievances and miseries, and pointed out the necessity of putting a stop to the oppression and avarice of their rulers. "The Neapolitan people," said he, "must pay no more taxes!" The people cried out, "Let Masaniello be our chief!"

The crowd now set itself in motion, with Masaniello at their head; it rolled onward, increasing its numbers at every step. Their rage first fell on the toll-houses and booths of the tax collectors, which were burned, and next on the houses and palaces of those who had farmed the taxes, or otherwise supported the obnoxious system. Armed with such weapons as they could procure from the gunsmiths and others, they proceeded to the viceroy's palace, forced their way in spite of the guards; and Masaniello and others, his companions, having reached the viceroy's presence, peremptorily demanded the abolition of all taxes.

The viceroy assented to this; but the tumult increasing, he tried to escape, was personally ill-treated, and at last contrived, by throwing money among the rioters, to withdraw himself into the castle. The palaces were emptied of their furniture, which was carried into the midst of the square, and there burnt by Masaniello's directions. He was now saluted by acclamation, as "Captain General of the Neapolitan people." A platform was immediately raised in the square, and he entered upon the duties of his office.

The revolution was soon complete, and Naples, the metropolis of many fertile provinces, the queen of many noble cities, the resort of princes, of cavaliers, and of heroes;—Naples, inhabited by more than six hundred thousand souls, abounding in all kinds of resources, glorying in its strength, and proud of its wealth—saw itself forced in one short day to yield to a man esteemed one of its meanest sons, such obedience as in all its history it had never before shown to the mightiest of its legitimate sovereigns.

In a few hours, the fisherman found himself at the head of one hundred and fifty thousand men; in a few hours, there was no will in Naples but his; and in a few hours, it was freed from all sorts of taxes and restored to its ancient privileges. In a short space, the fishing wand was exchanged for the truncheon of command; the sea-boy's jacket for cloth of silver and gold. He set about his new duties with astonishing vigor; he caused the town to be entrenched; he placed sentinels to guard it against danger from without, and he established a system of police within, which awed the worst banditti in the world, into fear.

Armies passed in review before him; even fleets owned his sway. He dispensed punishments and rewards with the like liberal hand; the bad he kept in awe; the disaffected he paralyzed; the wavering he resolved by exhortation; the bold were encouraged by incitements; the valiant were made more valiant by his approbation. Obeyed in whatever he commanded, gratified in whatever he desired, never was there a chief more absolute, never was an absolute chief, for a time, more powerful. He ordered that all the nobles and cavaliers should deliver up their arms to such officers as he should give commission to receive them. The order was obeyed. He ordered that all men of all ranks should go without cloaks or gowns, or wide cassocks, or any other sort of loose dress, under which arms might be concealed; nay, that even the women, for the same reason, should throw aside their farthingales, and tuck up their gowns somewhat high.

This order changed in an instant the whole fashions of the people; not even the proudest and the fairest of Naples' daughters daring to dispute, in the least, the pleasure of the people's idol. Nor was it over the high and noble alone, that he exercised this unlimited ascendancy. The fierce democracy were as acquiescent as the titled few. On one occasion, when the people in vast numbers were assembled, he commanded, with a loud voice, that every one present should, under the penalty of death, retire to his home. The multitude instantly dispersed. On another, he put his finger on his mouth, to command silence; in a moment, every voice was hushed. At a sign from him, all the bells tolled and the people shouted "*Vivas!*" at another, they all became mute.

Yet the reign of this prodigy of power was short, lasting only from the 7th till the 16th of July, 1647; when he perished, the victim of another political revolution. His sudden rise, and the multiplicity of affairs that crowded upon him, began to derange his intellect. He complained of sensations like that of boiling lead, in his head; he became suspicious, wavering and cruel. In a fit of frenzy he went to one of the churches and talked incoherently to the multitude. He was taken by the priests to an adjoining convent, and advised to rest and calm himself. After reposing for a time, he arose, and stood looking forth upon the tranquil bay of Naples, no doubt thinking of happier days, when, as a poor fisherman, he glided out contented upon its bosom—when all at once a cry was heard, of "Masaniello!" At the same instant armed men appeared at the cell door. "Here am I,—O, my people want me," said he. The discharge of guns was their only reply; and the victim fell, exclaiming, "Ungrateful traitors!" His head was now cut off, fixed on a pole, and carried to the viceroy, while the body was dragged through the streets and thrown into a ditch, by those who had followed it with acclamations a few hours before!

RIENZI.

Nicholas Gabrine de Rienzi was a native of Rome, and son of one of the lowest order of tavernkeepers. He was, however, well educated, and early distinguished himself by his talents and the elevation of his sentiments. The glory of ancient Rome excited his enthusiasm, and he soon came to be regarded by the people as destined to rescue them from the despotism of the aristocracy that ruled the city.

The pope, Clement VI., had removed the papal see from Rome to Avignon, in France, leaving the people under the sway of certain noble families, who exercised every species of brutal and insolent tyranny towards their inferiors. Rienzi saw this, and he felt all the indignation which a generous sympathy for the oppressed could excite. His sentiments being known, he was appointed, in 1346, among others, to proceed to Avignon, and exhort the pope to bring back the papal court to its original seat. He acted, on this occasion, with so much energy and eloquence, that the pope, though he refused compliance with the request, conferred upon him the office of apostolic notary, which, on his return, he executed with the strictest probity.

It appears that Rienzi had long meditated some great effort for the liberation of his countrymen. He now lost no opportunity to instruct the people in their rights, and stir up indignation against their oppressors. Having prepared men's minds for a change, and having secretly engaged persons of all orders in his designs, he proceeded to put them in execution. In April, 1347, Stephen Colonna, a nobleman, who was governor of Rome, being absent from the city, Rienzi secretly assembled his followers upon Mount Aventine, and, by an energetic speech, induced them all to subscribe an oath for the establishment of a new government, to be entitled the *Good Estate*.

Proceeding now with more boldness, another assembly was held in the capital; a constitution of fifteen articles was produced and ratified, and Rienzi was pronounced Tribune by acclamation, with the power of life and death, and all the attributes of sovereignty. Colonna returned, and threatened him with punishment; but the power had changed hands, and Colonna himself was obliged to fly. Rienzi proceeded in the exercise of his authority with strict justice. Some of the more culpable nobles were executed, and others banished.

The power of the new tribune was established, and his reputation extended throughout Italy. His friendship was solicited by kings and princes; the pope sanctioned his authority, and even Petrarch, the immortal poet, addressed him letters, which are still extant, bestowing upon him eloquent praise, and urging him to perseverance in his glorious career. But, unhappily, there was a weakness in Rienzi's character, which disqualified him for this giddy elevation. Intoxicated with the possession of supreme power, and the flatteries bestowed upon him, he became capricious and tyrannical, and, in short, commenced a reign of terror.

His descent was as rapid as his rise; soon finding that he had lost the affection of the people, in 1348, he withdrew for safety to Naples. Two years after, during a public jubilee at Rome, he secretly returned to that city, but being discovered, he withdrew to Prague. He now fell into the hands of Pope Clement, who kept him in prison for three years. His successor, Innocent VI., caused him to be released, and sent him to Rome, to oppose another demagogue, named Boroncelli.

The Romans received him with joy, and he suddenly recovered his former authority. But he was still a tyrant, and after a turbulent administration of a few months, another sedition was excited against him, and he was stabbed to the heart. The fickle people now bestowed every indignity upon the senseless remains of him, whom they had almost worshipped a few weeks before. Such was the career of Rienzi, who was endowed with noble sentiments and remarkable eloquence, but was deficient in that steadiness of mind and firmness of principle, which are necessary to the just exercise of unlimited sway.

SELKIRK.

ALEXANDER SELKIRK was born at Largo, Scotland, in 1676, and bred to the sea. Having engaged in the half piratical, half exploring voyages in the American seas, into which the spirit of adventure had led so many Englishmen, he quarrelled with his captain, one Straddling, by whom he was left ashore, September, 1704, on the uninhabited island of Juan

Fernandez, with a few books, his nautical instruments, a knife, boiler, axe, gun, powder and ball. These constituted his whole equipment.

The island of Juan Fernandez lies in the Pacific Ocean, and is about three hundred and thirty miles west of Chili. It is twelve miles long and six wide. It is beautifully diversified with hills and valleys, and has been long resorted to for water, fruits, and game, by vessels navigating the Pacific Ocean. Upon this island, Selkirk now found himself alone. He saw the vessel depart with sadness and sickness at heart. His emotions of terror and loneliness overwhelmed him for a time, and he remained in a state of stupor and inactivity.

But these feelings gradually faded away, and though his situation was appalling, he concluded to make the best of it. He now set about erecting himself two huts, one of which served him for a kitchen, the other for a dining-room and bed-chamber. The pimento wood supplied him with fire and candles, burning very clearly, and yielding a most fragrant smell. The roofs of his huts were covered with long grass.

The island was stocked with wild goats. He supplied himself with meat by shooting these, so long as his ammunition lasted. When this was exhausted, he caught them by running; and so practised was he at last in this exercise, that the swiftest goat on the island was scarcely a match for him. When his clothes were worn out, he made himself a covering of goat-skins. After a short space, he had no shoes, and was obliged to go barefoot; his feet, however, became so callous, that he did not seem to need them.

Soon after he had become settled in his hut, he was annoyed by rats, which became so bold as to gnaw his clothes and nibble at his feet while he slept. However, the same ships which had supplied the island with rats, had left some cats ashore. Some of these, Selkirk domesticated, and the rats were taught to keep themselves at a distance. He caught also some young goats, which he reared, and amused himself by teaching them to dance and perform many other tricks. During his stay upon the island, Selkirk caught and killed nearly five hundred goats. A few he set at liberty, having cropped their ears. Thirty years after, Lord Anson's crew shot a goat upon the island, and found its ears marked in the manner described.

Selkirk generally enjoyed good health, but in one case he nearly lost his life by accident. In the eager pursuit of a goat among the mountains, he fell over a precipice, and lay there for some time in a state of insensibility. On recovering his senses, he found the animal which had caused his fall, lying dead beneath him.

Selkirk often saw vessels pass by the island, and made frequent, but vain attempts to hail them. At length, after he had lived here in perfect solitude for four years and four months, he was taken off by an English vessel, commanded by Captain Rogers. This occurred in February, 1709. Although he felt great joy at his deliverance, he still manifested much difficulty in recovering his speech, and in returning to such food as he found on board the ship. It was a long time before he could again accustom himself to shoes.

Captain Rogers made him a mate of his ship, and he returned to England in 1711. It has been supposed that he gave his papers to De Foe, who wove, out of his adventures, the admirable story of Robinson Crusoe. It appears, however, that he made little use of Selkirk's narrative, beyond the mere idea of a man living alone for several years upon an uninhabited island.

JOHN LAW.

THIS celebrated financial projector was born at Edinburgh, in April, 1671. His father was a goldsmith, and gave him a liberal education. He made considerable progress in polite literature, but his favorite study was finance as connected with national prosperity.

In 1694, he visited London, where his talents and accomplishments gained him access to the first circles. He possessed an easy address, with an elegant person, and being a favorite with the fair, he acquired some notoriety in fashionable life. He became involved in a duel, in which he killed his antagonist, and was consequently committed to prison. He contrived, however, to escape, and took refuge on the continent.

In 1700, he returned to Edinburgh, where he broached a scheme for removing the difficulties which then existed in consequence of the scarcity of money and the failure of the banks. Having confounded currency with credit, he adopted the notion that paper money, equal to the whole property of the nation, might safely be issued. Upon this egregious error, his project was founded, and was, of course, rejected by his wary and sagacious countrymen.

Law now visited the principal cities of Europe; his address gaining him admittance to the highest circles in all countries. He finally settled in Paris, and was there during the regency of the Duke of Orleans, as guardian of Louis XV. The government of France was then on the verge of bankruptcy, in consequence of the enormous expenditures of Louis XIV. Law now brought forward his schemes for a free supply of money, and they were seized upon with avidity.

He established a bank, for which, a royal charter was granted in 1718. It was first composed of twelve hundred shares, of three thousand livres each, but the number was afterwards increased and the price reduced. This bank became the office at which all public moneys were received. A Mississippi company was also attached to it, which had grants of land in Louisiana, and which was expected to realize immense sums by planting and commerce. One privilege after another was granted, until the prospects of advantage appeared to be so great that crowds came forward to make investments in the stock of what was called the Mississippi Company.

Thousands embarked in the scheme with enthusiasm. The shares were greedily bought up, and such was the rage for speculation, that even the unimproved parts of the new colony were actually sold for thirty thousand livres the square league! But the delusion did not stop here. In consequence of the company promising an annual dividend of two hundred livres per share, the price rose from five hundred and fifty to five thousand livres, and the mania for purchasing the stock spread over the nation like a tempest. Every class, clergy and laity, peers and plebeians, statesmen and princes,— nay, even ladies, who had, or could produce money for that purpose, turned stock-jobbers, outbidding each other with such avidity, that, in November, 1719, after some fluctuations, the price of shares rose to more than sixty times the sum for which they were originally sold!

Law was now at the pinnacle of his fame. He was considered a man of so great consequence, that his levee was constantly crowded by persons of eminence, who flocked to Paris to partake of the golden shower. On one occasion, he was taken sick, and such was the feverish state of the public mind, that the shares of the company immediately fell nearly eight per cent., and, upon the rumor of his convalescence, immediately rose, even beyond their former price.

But the mighty bubble, now inflated to the utmost, was about to burst. On the 21st of April, 1719, a royal order, under pretence of a previous depreciation of the value of coin, declared it necessary to reduce the nominal value of bank notes to one half, and the shares of the Mississippi Company from nine thousand to five thousand livres. It is not possible to describe the calamitous effects which immediately followed, throughout France. The bank notes could not be circulated for more than one tenth of their nominal value. Another order was issued, intended to counteract the effect of the first; but the charm was broken, and nothing could restore the confidence of the public. All was panic and confusion. Bank notes were refused in all transactions of business, and even a royal order, commanding their acceptance, was of no avail. The public alarm was carried to its height, and at last the bank suspended the payment of its notes.

The splendid scheme had now exploded; the institution was bankrupt, and the shares were utterly worthless. Thousands of families, once wealthy, were suddenly reduced to indigence. The indignation of the public was speedily turned against the chief instrument of these delusions, and Law found it necessary to seek safety by flight. He resided, for some time, in different places in Germany, and settled at length in Venice, where he died, in 1729.

TRENCK.

FREDERICK, BARON TRENCK was born in Konigsberg, in Prussia, on the 16th February, 1726, of one of the most ancient families of the country. His father, who died in 1740, with the rank of major-general of cavalry, bestowed particular care on the education of his son, and sent him, at the age of thirteen, to the university of his native city, where he made a rapid progress in his studies. He soon began to manifest that impetuous disposition and those violent passions, which were probably the source of his subsequent misfortunes. By the time he was sixteen, he had been engaged in three duels, in each of which he wounded his antagonist.

He went into the army at an early period, and soon obtained the notice and favor of the king. When arrived at manhood, he was remarkable for personal beauty and mingled grace and dignity of bearing. Being stationed at Berlin, he became acquainted with the Princess Amelia, sister of Frederick the Great, and a mutual attachment followed. This became a subject of conversation, and soon reached the ears of Frederick. He warned Trenck to break off his intercourse with the princess; but this being unheeded, the king sent him to Glatz, under some pretext, and caused him to be imprisoned.

His confinement soon became insupportable to his impatient temper, and he resolved to avail himself of the first opportunity of escape. The window of his apartment looked toward the city, and was ninety feet from the ground, in the tower of the citadel. With a notched penknife, he sawed through three iron bars, and with a file, procured from one of the officers, he effected a passage through five more, which barricaded the windows. This done, he cut his leathern portmanteau into thongs, sewed them end to end, added the sheets of his bed, and safely descended from the astonishing height.

The night was dark, and everything seemed to promise success; but a circumstance he had never considered was, that he had to wade through moats full of mud, before he could enter the city. He sunk up to the knees, and, after long struggling and incredible efforts to extricate himself, he was obliged to call the sentinel, and desire him to go and tell the governor that Trenck was stuck fast in the ditch!

After the failure of several other attempts, he finally succeeded in effecting his escape, and fled to Vienna. From thence, he went to St. Petersburg, where he was received with the highest distinction, and the road to honors and emoluments was laid open before him. But at this period, the death of a wealthy cousin in Austria, induced him to return thither. Here, an immense property slipped through his hands, in consequence of some legal flaws.

In 1754, his mother died, from whose estate he received a considerable sum. With a view to the settlement of her affairs, he went to Dantzic, not permitting his name to be known. He was, however, betrayed into the hands of Frederick's officers, and being conveyed to the castle of Magdeburg, was immured in a dungeon, and loaded with irons.

Round his neck was a broad band of iron, to the ring of which his chains were suspended. These were of such weight, that, when he stood up, he was obliged to sustain them with his hands, to prevent being strangled. Various other massive irons were riveted to his body, and the whole were fastened to a thick staple, which was set in the stone wall. Under this staple was a seat of bricks, and on the opposite side a water jug. Beneath his feet was a tombstone, with the name of Trenck carved over a death's head.

His confinement in this dreadful cell continued for nine years and five months. In vain did he attempt to bribe the sentinels, and by other ingenious means, to effect his escape. His furniture consisted of a bedstead, a mattress, and a small stove. His food was a pound and a half of mouldy bread and a jug of water a day. He was permitted to hold no intercourse with any one except his keepers, and even these returned no answer to his thousand questions.

Such, however, were the vigor of his constitution and the elasticity of his spirits, that, amid the gloomy horrors of his prison, he seemed still to seek amusement by the exertion of his talents. He composed verses, and, having no ink, wrote them with his blood. He also carved curious emblems upon tin cups with his knife. His great ingenuity excited the attention of many persons of rank, particularly the Empress Maria Theresa, who ordered her minister to employ all his influence at the court of Berlin to obtain his enlargement.

The Baron, in his Life, relates the following curious anecdote:—"I tamed a mouse so perfectly that the little animal was continually playing with me, and used to eat out of my mouth. One night it skipped about so much, that the sentinels heard a noise, and made their report to the officer of the guard. As the garrison had been changed at the peace, and as I had not been able to form, at once, so close a connection with the officers of the regular troops, as I had done with those of the militia, an officer of the former, after ascertaining the truth of the report with his own ears, sent to inform the commanding officer that something extraordinary was going on in my prison.

"The town major arrived, in consequence, early in the morning, accompanied by locksmiths and masons. The floor, the walls, my chains, my body, everything, in short, was strictly examined. Finding all in order, they asked me the cause of last evening's bustle. I had heard the mouse myself, and told them frankly by what the noise had been occasioned. They desired me to call my little favorite; I whistled, and the mouse immediately leaped on my shoulder. I solicited its pardon, but the officer of the guard took it into his possession, promising, however, on his word of honor, to give it to a lady who would take great care of it. Turning it afterwards loose in his chamber, the mouse, who knew nobody but me, soon disappeared and hid itself in a hole.

"At the usual hour of visiting my prison, when the officers were just going away, the poor little animal darted in, climbed up my legs, seated itself on my shoulder, and played a thousand tricks to express the joy it felt at seeing me again. Every one was astonished and wished to have it. The major, to terminate the dispute, carried it away and gave it to his wife, who had a light cage made for it; but the mouse refused to eat, and a few days afterwards was found dead."

Trenck was at length released, and soon after married an amiable lady, by whom he had eleven children. On the death of Frederick the Great, his successor granted him a passport to Berlin, and restored his confiscated estates, which he had not enjoyed for forty-two years. He soon set off for Konigsburg, where he found his brother, who was very sick, waiting for him with impatience, and who adopted his children as his heirs. He was also received by all his friends with testimonies of joy. Here, it would appear, that Trenck might have spent the remainder of his days, in peace and quiet, but his restless disposition again made him the football of fortune. After many vicissitudes, he terminated his career in obscurity, and died in 1797.

JOHN DUNN HUNTER.

ABOUT the year 1822, there appeared at New York a young man, of small stature, light hair, light eyes, and in every respect of ordinary appearance, who told of himself a strange and interesting story, which was briefly this.

At an early period of his childhood, he, with two other white children, living on the farthest bound of the western settlements, were one day carried off by a party of Indians, probably Kickapoos. One of the children was killed before his eyes, and he was soon separated from the other. He was carried to a considerable distance by the Indians, who at last arrived at their hunting grounds. He became gradually reconciled to his situation, and, though he was occasionally taunted by being *white*, he was finally regarded as one of the tribe.

He continued to live among the Indians for many years; travelled with them in their migrations over the vast western wilds, visited the borders of the Pacific Ocean, and shared in the wild adventures of Indian life. He came, with his Indian friends, at last, to the Osage settlements on the Arkansas, where he found some white traders, among whom was a Colonel Watkins, who treated him with kindness, and sought to persuade him to leave the

Indians, and return to civilized life. Such, however, was his attachment to his adopted friends, that he rejected these suggestions.

Soon after, however, under the influence of intoxication, his Indian friends having laid a deep scheme for murdering Colonel Watkins and his party of hunters, the hero of our story deserted his tribe, and gave timely notice to Watkins, thus saving his life, and that of his friends.

Though his mind was greatly agitated by a feeling of self-disgust for the treachery he had committed toward his Indian brethren, he continued with the party of Watkins for a time, and descended the Arkansas river with them, nearly to its junction with the Mississippi. Here he left them, having made up his mind to join some Indian tribe which might not be acquainted with his breach of faith to the band of Osages, with whom he had lived so long.

Being supplied with a rifle and plenty of ammunition, he struck into the wilderness in a northerly direction, and pursued his wanderings alone, amid the boundless solitude. In the volume which he afterwards published, he thus describes this portion of his adventures:—

"The hunting season for furs had now gone by, and the time and labor necessary to procure food for myself, was very inconsiderable. I knew of no human being near me; my only companions were the grazing herds, the rapacious animals that preyed on them, the beaver and other animals that afforded pelts, and birds, fish and reptiles. Notwithstanding this solitude, many sources of amusement presented themselves to me, especially after I had become somewhat familiarized to it.

"The country around was delightful, and I roved over it almost incessantly, in ardent expectation of falling in with some party of Indians, with whom I might be permitted to associate myself. Apart from the hunting that was essential to my subsistence, I practised various arts to take fish, birds, and small game; frequently bathed in the river, and took great pleasure in regarding the dispositions and habits of such animals as were presented to my observation.

"The conflicts of the male buffaloes and deer, the attack of the latter on the rattlesnake, the industry and ingenuity of the beaver in constructing its dam, and the attacks of the panther on its prey, afforded much interest, and engrossed much time. Indeed, I have lain for half a day at a time, in the shade, to witness the management and policy observed by the ants in storing up their food, the manœuvres of the spider in taking its prey, the artifice of the mason-fly in constructing and storing its clayey cells, and the voraciousness and industry of the dragon-fly to satisfy its appetite.

"In one instance, I vexed a rattlesnake, till it bit itself, and subsequently saw it die from the poison of its own fangs. I also saw one strangled in the wreathed folds of its inveterate enemy—the black snake. But, in the midst of this extraordinary employment, my mind was far from being satisfied. I looked back with the most painful reflections on what I had been, and on what sacrifices I had made, merely to become an outcast, to be hated and despised by those I sincerely loved and esteemed. But, however much I was disposed to be dissatisfied and quarrel with myself, the consolation of the most entire conviction that I had acted rightly, always followed, and silenced my self-upbraidings.

"The anxiety and regrets about my nation, country and kindred, for a long time held paramount dominion over all my feelings; but I looked unwaveringly to the Great Spirit, in whom experience had taught me to confide, and the tumultuous agitations of my mind gradually subsided into a calm; I became satisfied with the loneliness of my situation, could lie down to sleep among the rocks, ravines, and ferns, in careless quietude, and hear the wolf and panther prowling around me; and I could almost feel the venomous reptiles seeking shelter and repose under my robe, with sensations bordering on indifference.

"In one of my excursions, while sitting in the shade of a large tree, situated on a gentle declivity, with a view to procure some mitigation from the oppressive heat of the mid-day sun, I was surprised by a tremendous rushing noise. I sprang up, and discovered a herd, I believe, of a thousand buffaloes, running at full speed, directly towards me; with a view, as I supposed, to beat off the flies, which, at this season, are inconceivably troublesome to those animals.

"I placed myself behind the tree, so as not to be seen, not apprehending any danger, because they ran with too great rapidity, and too closely together, to afford any one of them an opportunity of injuring me, while protected in this manner.

"The buffaloes passed so near me on both sides that I could have touched several of them, merely by extending my arm. In the rear of the herd, was one on which a huge panther had fixed, and was voraciously engaged in cutting off the muscles of the neck. I did not discover this circumstance till it had nearly passed beyond rifle-shot distance, when I discharged my piece, and wounded the panther. It instantly left its hold on the buffalo, and bounded, with great rapidity, towards me. On witnessing the result of my shot, the apprehensions I suffered can hardly be imagined. I had, however, sufficient presence of mind to retreat, and secrete myself behind the trunk of the tree, opposite to its approaching direction. Here, solicitous for what possibly might be the result of my unfortunate shot, I prepared both my knife and tomahawk for what I supposed would be a deadly conflict with the terrible animal.

"In a few moments, however, I had the satisfaction to hear it in the branches of the tree over my head. My rifle had just been discharged, and I entertained fears that I could not reload it without discovering and exposing myself to the fury of its destructive rage. I looked into the tree with the utmost caution, but could not perceive it, though its groans and vengeance-breathing growls told me that it was not far off, and also what I had to expect in case it should discover me.

"In this situation, with my eyes almost constantly directed upwards to observe its motions, I silently loaded my rifle, and then, creeping softly round the trunk of the tree, saw my formidable enemy resting on a considerable branch, about thirty feet from the ground, with his side fairly exposed. I was unobserved, took deliberate aim, and shot it through the heart. It made a single bound from the tree to the earth, and died in a moment afterwards.

"I reloaded my rifle before I ventured to approach it, and even then not without some apprehension. I took its skin, and was, with the assistance of fire and smoke, enabled to preserve and dress it. I name this circumstance, because it afterwards afforded a source of some amusement; for I used frequently to array myself in it, as near as possible to the costume and form of the original, and surprise the herds of buffaloes, elk and deer, which, on my approach, uniformly fled with great precipitation and dread.

"On several occasions, when I waked in the morning, I found a rattlesnake coiled up close alongside of me: some precaution was necessarily used to avoid them. In one instance, I lay quiet till the snake saw fit to retire; in another, I rolled gradually and imperceptibly away, till out of its reach; and in another, where the snake was still more remote, but in which we simultaneously discovered each other, I was obliged, while it was generously warning me of the danger I had to fear from the venomous potency of its fangs, to kill it with my tomahawk."

After Hunter had been engaged in roving about in this manner for several months, hoping to meet with some party of Indians to whom he might attach himself, he met with a company of French hunters, whom he accompanied to Flee's settlement, on the White river. From this point, after a stay of some months, in which he acquired a good deal of credit for cures which he performed by means of Indian remedies, he set out on a hunting expedition, during which he collected a large quantity of furs. These he sold to a Yankee, for 650 dollars, as he supposed, but, being ignorant on the subject of money, he found, on having the cash counted, that it was only 22 dollars!

This took place at Maxwell's fort, on the White river. Disgusted with the white people, by this act of plunder, he determined to quit them forever, and set off again to join the Indians. He was, however, diverted from his purpose, and went with a hunting party up the west fork of the river St. Francis. Spending the season here, he returned, and making his way down the Mississippi, sold his furs for 1100 dollars. Thence he proceeded as a boatman to New Orleans, where his mind was greatly astonished at the scenes he beheld, the streets, the houses, the wharves, ships, &c.

He retraced his steps, and came to Cape Girardeau, in Missouri, where he remained some time, acquiring the rudiments of the English language. His acquaintances had given him the name of Hunter, because of his expertness and success in the chase. His Christian name was adopted, as he says in his book, from the following circumstance. "As Mr. John Dunn, a gentleman of high respectability, of Cape Girardeau county, state of Missouri, had treated me in every respect more like a brother or a son than any other individual had, since my association with the white people, I adopted his for that of my distinctive, and have since been known by the name of John Dunn Hunter." It is important for the reader to mark this passage, for important results afterwards turned upon it.

He now spent two or three years, a part of the time at school, making, however, several expeditions to New Orleans, to dispose of furs he had either taken in hunting or obtained by purchase. At last, in the autumn of 1821, he crossed the Alleganies, and entered upon a new career. So far, his story is told by himself, in his book, which we shall notice hereafter.

On his way, Hunter paid a visit to Mr. Jefferson, who received him kindly, and, taking a strong interest in his welfare, gave him letters of introduction to several persons at Washington. Hunter went thither, and, passing on, came to Philadelphia, and at last to New York, everywhere exciting a lively interest, by the remarkable character of his story, and the manner in which he related it. He was found to be well-informed as to many things, then little known, respecting the western country; he was, accordingly, much sought after, patronized and flattered, especially by persons distinguished for science and wealth. He was, in short, a lion. The project was soon suggested, that he should write a book, detailing his adventures, and giving an account of the Indians, and the Indian country, as far as he was acquainted with these subjects. A subscription was started, and readily filled with a long list of great names. The book was written by Mr. Edward Clark, and, in 1823, it was published, under the title of "Manners and Customs of the several Indian Tribes located west of the Mississippi, &c."

This work, written in a clever style, detailed the wonderful life and adventures of the hero, and gave a view of the Far West—the country, the animals, the plants; and it described the Indian tribes, their numbers, character, customs, &c. It also gave an account of their system of medicine, and their practice of surgery. The book was well received, and Hunter was borne along upon the full tide of public favor.

And now, another view was opened to him. It was suggested that he should go to England, and publish his work there. Taking letters from several men of the highest standing, and especially one to the Duke of Sussex, from Mr.

Jefferson, as we are informed, he crossed the Atlantic, and made his appearance in the great metropolis. The career upon which he now entered, affords a curious piece of history.

Hunter's letters, of course, secured him the favor and kind offices of some of the leading men in London. His book was immediately published and heralded forth by the press, as one of the most remarkable productions of the day. The information it contained was treated as a revelation of the most interesting facts, and the tale of the hero was regarded as surpassing that of Robinson Crusoe, in point of interest.

Hunter was a man of extraordinary endowments, and sustained the part he had to play with wonderful consistency. But all this would hardly account for his success, without considering another point. In London, as well among the high as the low, there is a yearning desire for excitement. Imprisoned in a vast city, and denied companionship with the thousand objects which occupy the mind and heart in the country, they go about crying, "Who will show us any new thing?" Thus it is, that, in a crowded street, there is always a mob ready to collect, like vultures to the carcass, around every accident or incident that may happen: and these seem to consist of persons who have no profession but to see what is going on.

In high life, this passion for novelty is more refined, but it is equally craving. There are thousands in the circles of rank and fashion, who, having no business to occupy them, no cares, no sources of hope and fear, are like travellers athirst in a desert; and to them, a new scandal, a new fashion, a late joke, a strange animal, a queer monster, is an oasis, greatly to be coveted. One quality this novelty must have; it must, in some way or other, belong to "good society"—my Lord, or my Lady, must have a finger in it: they must, at least, patronize it, so that in naming it, the idea of rank may be associated with it.

Such a new thing was John Dunn Hunter. He was, supposing his story to be true, remarkable for his adventures. There was something exceedingly captivating to the fancy in the idea of a white man, who had lived so long with savages, as to have been transformed into a savage himself: beside, there was a mystery about him. Who was his father?—who his mother?

What a tale of romance lay in these pregnant inquiries, and what a beautiful development might yet be in the womb of time!

Nor was this all: Hunter, as we have said, was a man of talent. Though small and mean in his personal appearance, his manner was remarkable, and his demeanor befitted his story. He had taken lodgings in Warwick street, and occupied the very rooms which Washington Irving had once inhabited. Another American author, of no mean fame, was his fellow-lodger. He held free intercourse with all Americans who came to London. He sought their society, and, in the height of his power, he loved to exercise it in their behalf, and to their advantage.

In dress, Hunter adopted the simplest garb of a gentleman; in conversation, he was peculiar. He said little till excited; he then spoke rapidly, and often as if delivering an oration. He was accustomed to inveigh against civilized society,—its luxuries and its vices,—and to paint in glowing hues the pleasures and virtues of savage life. He was very ingenious, and often truly eloquent. It was impossible, believing in the genuineness of his character and the sincerity of his motives, not to be touched by his wild enthusiasm.

It is easy to see, that such a man, unsuspected, introduced into society by the brother of the king, and patronized by the heads of the learned societies —launched upon the full tide of fashionable society, in the world's metropolis,—had a brilliant voyage before him. During the winter of 1823-4, Hunter was the lion of the patrician circles of London. There was a real strife even among countesses, duchesses, and the like, to signalize their parties by the presence of this interesting wonder. In considering whether to go to a ball, a soirée, or a jam, the deciding point of inquiry was, "Will Hunter be there?"—If so, "Yes."—If not, "No!"

Nothing could be more curious than to see this singular man, in the midst of a gorgeous party, where diamonds flashed and titles hung on every individual around him. He seemed totally indifferent to the scene; or, at least, unobservant of the splendors that encircled him. He was the special object of regard to the ladies. There was something quite piquant in his indifference. He seemed not to acknowledge the flatteries, that fell like showers of roses, and that too from the ruby lips and lustrous eyes of princes' daughters, thick upon him. He seldom sat down: he stood erect, and, even when encircled by ladies, gazed a little upward, and over them. He often answered a question without looking at the querist. Sometimes, though quite rarely, he was roused, and delivered a kind of speech. It was a great thing, if the oracle would but hold forth! The lass or lady who chanced to hear this, was but too happy. The burden of the oration was always nearly the same:—the advantages of simple savage life over civilization. It was strange to see those who were living on the pinnacle of artificial society, intoxicated with such a theme; yet, such was the art of the juggler, that even their fancy was captivated. Those who had been bred in the downy lap of luxury, were charmed with tales of the hardy chase and deadly encounter; those to whom the artifices of dress constituted more than half the pleasures of existence, delighted to dwell upon the simplicity of forest attire: those who gloried in the splendors of a city mansion,—halls, boudoirs, saloons, and conservatories,—thought how charming it would be to dwell beneath the wide canopy, or a deer-skin tent! Surely, such triumphs display the skill and power of a master.

During the winter of which we speak, Hunter's card-rack was crowded with cards, notes, and invitations, from lords and ladies of the very highest rank and fashion, in London. Many a fair hand indited and sent billets to him, that would have turned some loftier heads than his. On one occasion, by some accident, he had dislocated his shoulder. The next morning, Dr. Petingale, surgeon to the Duke of Sussex, called to see him, by command of his Grace, and delivered to him a long note of consolation. This note, from his Royal Highness, was somewhat in the style of Hannah More, and kindly suggested all the topics of comfort proper to such an hour of tribulation.

Hunter did not spend his whole time in fashionable dissipation. He visited the various institutions of London, and often with persons of the highest rank. He fell in with Robert Owen, of Lanarck, who had not yet been pronounced mad, and the two characters seemed greatly delighted with each other. Hunter seemed interested in the subject of education, and made this a frequent topic of discussion. He visited the infant school of Wilderspin, consisting of two hundred scholars, all of the lower classes. When he heard forty of these children, under three years of age, unite in singing "God save the King," his heart was evidently touched, and the tears gathered in his eyes. It is not one of the least curious facts in his history, that he patronized his countrymen, and was the means of establishing a portrait painter from

Kentucky, in his profession. He induced the Duke of Sussex, with whom he regularly dined once a week, to sit for him: the portrait was exhibited at Somerset House, and our artist was at once famous.

Hunter now took a tour to Scotland. In his way, he spent some weeks with Mr. Coke, of Norfolk, and experienced the noble hospitalities of that truly noble gentleman. He passed on to Scotland, where he excited a deep interest among such persons as the Duke of Hamilton, Sir Walter Scott, Mr. Jeffrey, and others of the highest eminence. The ladies, also, manifested the very liveliest sensations in his behalf.

During his stay in Scotland, he was invited to spend a few days at a charming seat, in the vicinity of Edinburgh. Thither he went. One day, as he was walking in the park with a fair lady, daughter of the proprietor, they came to an open space, through which a bright stream was running. At a particular point, and near the path of the ramblers, was a large rock, at the base of which the rivulet swept round, forming a small eddying pool. Over this the wild shrubs had gathered, growing luxuriously, as if escaped from the restraints of culture. Hunter paused, folded his arms, and gazed at the picturesque group of rock, shrub, and stream. The lady looked at him with interest. She hesitated, then gathered courage, and asked what it was that so moved him.

"Nothing! nothing!" said he, half starting, and passing on. "Nay, nay," said the fair one, "you must tell me." "Well, if I must," was the reply, "I must. You may think it foolish, yet such is the truth,—that little pool, gathered in the shelter of the rock and briar, reminds me of early days—of my childhood, and the forest. Past memories come over my bosom, like summer upon the snow; I think how I have often stooped at such a stream as this, and quenched my thirst, with a relish nothing can now bestow. I feel an emotion I can hardly resist; it seems to call me from these scenes, this voluptuous, yet idle life. I have a sense of wrong, of duty neglected, of happiness missed, which makes me sad even in such a place as this, and with society like yours."

By this time Hunter had framed a design, either real or pretended, of doing some great thing for the Indians. He insisted that the attempt to civilize them at once, was idle and fallacious; he proposed, therefore, to select some spot along the banks of the Wabash, and which he represented as a wild kind of paradise, and here he would gather the Indians, and, adopting a system which might blend the life of the hunter with that of the cultivator, wile them gradually, and without shocking their prejudices, into civilization. This scheme he set forth as the great object of his wishes. He spoke of it frequently, and in Edinburgh, especially, delighted his hearers with his enthusiastic eloquence in dilating upon the subject. No one suspected his sincerity, and the greatest men in Scotland avowed and felt the deepest interest in his project.

The summer came, and Hunter went back to London. He now announced his intention to return to America: still, he lingered for several months. His friends noticed that he was dejected, yet he assigned no cause for this. Presents were made to him, and hints of assistance, to further his scheme of Indian civilization, were suggested. He availed himself of none of these advantages, save that he accepted a watch, richly jewelled, from the Duke of Sussex, and a splendid set of mathematical instruments, from Mr. Coke, of Norfolk. He also borrowed a hundred pounds of a friend. He took his farewell of London, and bearing with him the best wishes of all who had known him on that side of the Atlantic, he embarked at Liverpool for America.

Immediately after his arrival, he hastened to the south, spent a few days at New Orleans, and pushed into the wilds bordering upon Texas. In some way, he excited the jealousy of the Indians, who resolved to take his life. On a journey through the wilderness, he was attended by an Indian guide. Having occasion to pass a river, he stopped a moment in the middle of it, to let his horse drink. The guide was behind: obedient to his orders, he lifted his carbine, and shot Hunter through the back. He fell, a lifeless corpse, into the stream, and was borne away, as little heeded as a forest leaf.

Such are the facts, as we have been able to gather them, in respect to this remarkable man. The writer of this article saw him in London, and the incidents related of him while he was in England and Scotland, are stated upon personal knowledge. The events subsequent to his departure are derived from current rumor. The question has often been asked, What was the real character of John Dunn Hunter? That he was, to some extent, an impostor, can hardly be doubted. Mr. Duponceau, of Philadelphia, examined into some Indian words which Hunter had given him, and found them to be fabrications. Mr. John Dunn, of Missouri, mentioned by Hunter as his friend and benefactor, was written to, and he declared that he had known no such person. These facts, with others, were laid before the public in the North American Review, and were regarded as fatal to the character of Hunter. The common judgment has been, that he was wholly an impostor; we incline, however, to a different opinion.

We believe that the story of his early life, was, in the main, correct;[B] that he did not originally intend any deception; that he came to New York with honest intentions, but that the flatteries he received led him by degrees to expand his views, and finally drew him into a deliberate career of fraud. So long as he was in the tide of prosperity abroad, he did not seem to reflect, and glided down contented with the stream: when the time came that he must return, his real situation presented itself, and weighed upon his spirits. It is to be remarked, however, that, even in this condition, he availed himself of no opportunities to amass money, which he might have done to the amount of thousands. These facts, at war with the supposition that he was a mere impostor, seem to show that he had still some principle of honor left, and some hope as to his future career. At all events, he was a man of extraordinary address, and his story shows how high a course of duplicity may elevate a man, yet only to hurl him down the farther and the more fatally, upon the sharp rocks of retribution.

CASPER HAUSER.

In the year 1828, a great sensation was created throughout the civilized world, by the story of Casper Hauser. This, as it appears, was in substance as follows:—

On the 20th May, in the year above named, as a citizen of Nuremburg, in Bavaria, was proceeding along one of the streets, he happened to see a young man in the dress of a peasant, who was standing like one intoxicated, attempting to move forward, yet appearing hardly to have command of his legs. On the approach of the citizen, this stranger held out to him a letter directed to a well-known and respectable military officer, living in Nuremburg.

As the house of this person lay in the direction of the citizen's walk, he took the youth thither with him. When the servant opened the door, the stranger put the letter into his hand, uttering some unintelligible words. The various questions which were asked, as to his name, whence he came, &c., he seemed not to comprehend. He appeared excessively fatigued, staggered as if exhausted, and pointed to his feet, shedding tears, apparently from pain. As he seemed to be suffering from hunger, a piece of meat was given to him, but scarcely had he tasted it, when he spat it out, and shuddered as if with abhorrence. He manifested the same aversion to beer. He ate some bread and drank water, with signs of satisfaction.

Meantime, all attempts to gain any information from him were fruitless. To every question he answered with the same unintelligible jargon. He seemed to hear without understanding, and to see without perceiving. He shed many tears, and his whole language seemed to consist of moans and unintelligible sounds.

The letter to the officer, above mentioned, contained no satisfactory information. It stated that the writer was a poor day-laborer, with a family of ten children; that the bearer had been left with him in October, 1812, and he had never since been suffered to leave his house: that he had received a Christian education, been baptized, &c. He was sent to the officer with the request that he might be taken care of till seventeen years old, and then be made a trooper, and placed in the sixth regiment, as his father had been of that corps. This letter was supposed, of course, to be designed to mislead, and no reliance was placed upon it.

The officer, suspecting some imposition, sent the stranger to the police. To all inquiries the latter replied as before, displaying a kind of childish simplicity, and awkward dulness. He was continually whimpering, and pointing to his feet. While he had the size of a young man, his face had the expression of a child. When writing materials were placed before him, he took the pen with alacrity, and wrote *Kaspar Hauser*. This so contrasted with his previous signs of ignorance and dulness, as to excite suspicions of imposture, and he was therefore committed to a tower used for the confinement of rogues and vagabonds. In going to this place, he sank down, groaning at every step.

The body of Caspar seemed perfectly formed, but his face bore a decided aspect of vulgarity. When in a state of tranquillity, it was either destitute of expression, or had a look of brutish indifference. The formation of his face, however, changed in a few months, and rapidly gained in expression and animation. His feet bore no marks of having been confined by shoes, and were finely formed; the soles were soft as the palms of his hands. His gait was a waddling, tottering progress, groping with his hands as he went, and often falling at the slightest impediment. He could not, for a long time, go up and down stairs without assistance. He used his hands with the greatest awkwardness. In all these respects, however, he rapidly improved.

Caspar Hauser soon ceased to be considered either an idiot or an impostor. The mildness, good nature, and obedience he displayed, precluded the idea that he had grown up with the beasts of the forest. Yet he was destitute of words, and seemed to be disgusted with most of the customs and habits of civilized life. All the circumstances combined to create a belief that he had been brought up in a state of complete imprisonment and seclusion, during the previous part of his existence.

He now became an object of general interest, and hundreds of persons came to see him. He could be persuaded to taste no other food than bread and water. Even the smell of most articles of food was sufficient to make him shudder. When he first saw a lighted candle, he appeared greatly delighted, and unsuspectingly put his fingers into the blaze. When a mirror was shown him, he looked behind to find the image it reflected. Like a child, he greedily reached for every glittering object, and cried when any desired thing was denied him. His whole vocabulary seemed hardly to exceed a dozen words, and that of ross (horse) answered for all quadrupeds, such as horses, dogs, and cats. When, at length, a wooden horse was given as a plaything, it seemed to effect a great change in him; his spirits revived, and his lethargy and indifference were dissipated. He would never eat or drink without first offering a portion to his horse.

His powers seemed now to be rapidly developed; he soon quitted his toy, and learned to ride the living horse with astonishing rapidity. He, however, was greatly oppressed, as he acquired knowledge, at discovering how much inferior he was in knowledge to those around him, and this led him to express the wish that he could go back to the hole in which he had always been confined. From his repeated statements, now that he had learned to speak, it appeared that he had been, from his earliest recollections, confined in a narrow space, his legs extended forward upon the floor, and his body upright; and here, without light, and without the power of locomotion, he had remained for years. The date or period of his confinement he knew not, for in his dungeon there was no sunrise or sunset, to mark the lapse of time. When he awoke from sleep, he found some bread and water at his side; but who ministered to his wants, he knew not; he never saw the face of his attendant, who never spoke to him, except in some unintelligible jargon. In his hole he had two wooden horses and some ribands as toys—and these afforded him his only amusement. One day had passed as another; he had no dreams; time run on, and life ebbed and flowed, with a dull and almost unconscious movement. After a time his keeper gave him a pencil, of which he learned the use; he was then partially taught to walk, and shortly after, was carried from his prison, a letter put into his hand, and he was left, as the beginning of our story finds him, in the streets of Nuremburg.

The journals were now filled with accounts of this mysterious young man. A suspicion was at last started that he was of high birth, and that important motives had led to the singular treatment he had received. He was himself haunted with the fear of assassination, from the idea that the circumstances which led to his incarceration, now that his story was known, might tempt his enemies to put a period to his life—thus seeking at once the removal of a hated object, and security against detection. His fears were at last partially realized; while he was under the care and protection of Professor Daumer, he was attacked and seriously wounded by a blow upon the forehead.

After this event, Earl Stanhope, who happened to be in that part of Germany, caused him to be removed to Anspach, where he was placed under the care of an able schoolmaster. Here his fears subsided; but in December, 1833, a stranger, wrapped in a large cloak, accosted him, under the pretence of having an important communication to make, and proposed a meeting. Caspar agreed, and they met in the palace garden, alone. The stranger drew some papers from beneath his cloak, and while Hauser was examining them, the russian stabbed him in the region of the heart. The wound did not prove immediately fatal. He was able to return home, and relate what had happened. Messengers were sent in pursuit of the assassin, but in vain. Hauser lingered three or four days—that is, till the 17th

December, 1833, when he died. On dissection, it appeared that the knife had pierced to the heart, making an incision in its outer covering, and slightly cutting both the liver and stomach. A reward of five thousand florins was offered by Lord Stanhope, for the discovery of the assassin, but without effect—nor was the mystery which involved Caspar's story ever fully unravelled.

Such was the tale of this extraordinary individual, as it appeared a few years ago. Since that period, the facts in the case have been carefully sifted, and the result is a settled conviction, that Hauser was an impostor; that the story of his confinement was a fabrication; that his pretended ignorance, his stupidity, his childishness, were but skilful acting to enforce his story; and, strange as it may appear, there is no good reason to doubt that the wounds he received, in both instances, were inflicted by himself. Such were the deliberate convictions of Earl Stanhope, and others who investigated the facts on the spot, and with the best advantages for the discovery of the truth. Caspar's motive for wounding himself doubtless was, to revive the flagging interest of the public in his behalf—a source of excitement he had so long enjoyed, as to feel unhappy without it. In the latter instance, he doubtless inflicted a severer wound than he intended, and thus put an undesigned period to his existence.

His story presents one of the most successful instances of imposture, on record. It appears probable that he was aided in his imposition by the narrative of Fuerbach, one of the judges of Bavaria, who adopted some theory on the subject, which he supported with gross, though perhaps undesigned misrepresentation. He published an interesting account of Hauser, in which he rather colored and exaggerated the facts, thus making the narrative far more wonderful than the reality would warrant. It was, doubtless, owing to these statements of Fuerbach, that an extraordinary interest in the case was everywhere excited; and it is highly probable that Hauser himself was encouraged to deeper and more extended duplicity, by the aid which the mistaken credulity of the judge afforded him, than, at first, he had meditated. He probably looked with surprise and wonder at the success of his trick, and marvelled at seeing himself suddenly converted from a poor German mechanic, as he doubtless was, into a prodigy and a hero—exciting a sensation throughout the four quarters of the globe. The whole story affords a good illustration of the folly of permitting the imagination to lead us in the investigation of facts, and the extended impositions that may flow from the want of exact and scrupulous veracity in a magistrate.

PSALMANAZAR.

GEORGE PSALMANAZAR was born about the year 1679. All that we know of his early history is from his own memoirs, which were published after his death; but they do not tell us his true name, nor that of his native country, though it is generally believed that he was born in the south of France. His education was excellent, probably obtained in some of the colleges of the Jesuits.

At an early period, he became a wandering adventurer, sometimes passing himself off as a pilgrim, then as a Japanese, and then as a native of Formosa —a large island lying to the east of China, and subject to that country. His extensive learning and various knowledge enabled him to sustain these and other disguises. Thus he travelled over several parts of Europe, France, Germany, and the Netherlands. He was by turns a soldier, a beggar, a menial, a monk; a preceptor, a Christian, a heathen, a man of all trades. At last, he came to Liege in Belgium, pretending to be a Formosan, converted to Christianity. Here he became acquainted with the chaplain of an English regiment, and was solemnly baptized.

He now went to London, and was kindly received by Bishop Compton, who gave him entertainment in his own house, and treated him with the utmost confidence. His great abilities and extraordinary story, seconded by the patronage of the bishop of London, gave him immediate currency with literary men, and he soon became the wonder of the day.

Psalmanazar played his part to admiration. He shunned, rather than sought, the notice of the public, and, avoiding meat, lived chiefly on fruits, and a simple vegetable diet. At the same time, he appeared to display the Christian characteristics, and devoted himself to study. He began to prepare a grammar of the Formosan language, which he finally completed. This was, of course, a fiction, yet he proceeded to translate the Church Catechism into this fabricated tongue. He finally wrote an extensive history of Formosa, which was also a fable; yet such was the reputation of the author, that it was received with general confidence, and speedily passed through several editions.

During this period, he had been sent to study at Oxford, where a controversy was carried on between his patrons, and Dr. Halley, Dr. Mead, and some others, in respect to his pretensions. Certain discrepancies were at last detected in his history of Formosa, and, in the result, Psalmanazar was completely exposed, and finally confessed his imposture. Soon after this, a moral change took place in him: he grew ashamed of his dishonorable courses, and determined to reform. He applied himself intensely to study, and, after a time, became engaged in literary pursuits, by which he earned an honest subsistence, and considerable reputation during the rest of his life. He died in London, in 1753.

He wrote for the large work, styled the Universal History, most of the parts concerning ancient history, except that of Rome, and his writings met with great success. He wrote a volume of essays on several scriptural subjects, a version of the Psalms, beside his own memoirs, already mentioned. He also wrote for the "Complete System of Geography," an article on the Island of Formosa, founded upon authentic information, as a reparation for the stories which he had palmed upon the public in his former account.

Psalmanazar is the name that he had assumed when he began his wandering life, and which he retained till his death. Of the sincerity of his piety, there can be no doubt. Dr. Johnson said that he never witnessed a more beautiful example of humility, and tranquil resignation, combined with an active discharge of duty, than was displayed by him during the latter portion of his life!

VALENTINE GREATRAKES.

THIS person, renowned in the annals of quackery, was born at Affane, in Ireland, in 1628. He received a good education at the classical free school of that town, and was preparing to enter Trinity College, Dublin, when the rebellion broke out, and his mother, with a family of several children, was obliged to fly to England for refuge.

Some years after, Valentine returned, but was so affected by the wretched state of his country, and the scenes of misery that were witnessed on every hand, that he shut himself up for a whole year, spending his time in moody contemplations. He afterwards became a lieutenant in the army, but in 1656, he retired to his estate in Affane, where he was appointed justice of the peace for the county of Cork.

Greatrakes was now married, and appears to have held a respectable station in society. About the year 1662, he began to conceive himself possessed of an extraordinary power of removing scrofula, or king's evil, by means of touching or stroking the parts affected, with his hands. This imagination he concealed for some time, but, at last, revealed it to his wife, who ridiculed the idea.

Having resolved, however, to make the trial, he began with one William Maher, who was brought to the house by his father, for the purpose of receiving some assistance from Mrs. Greatrakes, a lady who was always ready to relieve the sick and indigent, as far as lay in her power. This boy was sorely afflicted with the king's evil, but was to all appearance cured by Mr. Greatrakes' laying his hand on the parts affected. Several other persons having applied to him, to be cured, in the same manner, of different disorders, his efforts seemed to be attended with success, and he acquired considerable fame in his neighborhood.

His reputation now increased, and he was induced to go to England, where he gained great celebrity by his supposed cures. Several pamphlets were issued upon the subject; it being maintained by some that Greatrakes possessed a sanative quality inherent in his constitution; by others, that his cures were miraculous; and by others still, that they were produced merely by the force of imagination. The reality of the cures seemed to be admitted, and the reputation of the operator rose to a prodigious height; but, after a brief period, it rapidly declined, and the public became convinced that the whole excitement was the result of illusion. Greatrakes, himself, possessed a high character for humility, virtue and piety, and was doubtless the dupe of his own bewildered fancy. He died in 1680, having afforded the world a striking caution not to mistake recovery for cure, and not to yield to imagination and popular delusion, especially in respect to the pretended cure of diseases.

MATTHEW HOPKINS.

ABOUT 250 years ago, the reality of witchcraft was very generally admitted throughout Europe. The belief in the active agency of the Spirit of Evil in human affairs, had existed among Christians from the earliest period, and the legends of saints, their trials and temptations, in which the devil plays so important a part, served to extend and confirm these popular notions. At last, the direct agency of diabolical powers, and its open manifestation, was assumed, and, at the period of which we speak, was held to be a point of Christian faith. The pious Baxter considered the disbelief of witchcraft as equivalent to infidelity; the just and sagacious Sir Matthew Hale admitted its reality, and pronounced sentence against those who were convicted of it; and, alas! the pedantic king, James I. of England, wrote a book entitled, "Dæmonologia, or a Discourse on Witchcraft."

The purpose of this work was to prove the reality of witchcraft, its prevalence among mankind, its great enormity, and the means of its detection and punishment. Its effect was to extend the belief in witchcraft, and, of course, to multiply the apparent instances of its existence. The insane fancies of diseased minds, unusual phenomena of nature, and the artful machinery of designing malignity, ambition, or hypocrisy, were all laid at Satan's door. Of the horrors that followed, history furnishes a melancholy account. It is supposed that 30,000 persons were executed in England, from the year 1500 to 1722. The same dreadful delusion prevailed in other parts of Europe, and extended in due time to this country, and about the year 1692, twenty persons were executed in Salem, Massachusetts, for the crime of witchcraft.

During the period in which this fearful mania was prevalent in England, Matthew Hopkins, denominated Witch-Finder General, acted a conspicuous part. He pretended to be a great critic in special marks or signs of witchcraft. Moles, warts, scorbutic spots, were in his eyes teats to suckle imps, and were sufficient evidences to bring a victim to the halter. He was assisted by one John Stern, a kindred genius, and in the year 1644, 5 and 6, they brought a great number of poor wretches to the fatal tree. Matthew, himself, hung in one year no less than sixty reputed witches of his own county of Essex. He received twenty shillings a head from the public authorities for every witch he discovered. The old, the ignorant, and the indigent,—such as could neither plead their own cause nor hire an advocate, were the miserable victims of his credulity, avarice, and spleen.

When other evidences of guilt were wanting, Hopkins adopted the trial by water, which had been suggested by king James, who remarks that "as some persons have renounced their baptism by water, so water refuses to receive them." Those accused of diabolical practices, therefore, were thrown into a pond. If they floated or swam, according to king James' notion the water refused to receive them, and they were therefore guilty. These were consequently taken out and burnt, or hung. If they were innocent, they sunk, and were only drowned.

Suspicion was at last turned against Hopkins himself, and the ordeal of swimming was applied in his own case. In consequence of this experiment, he was convicted and executed as a wizard. An allusion to this extraordinary character is made in the third canto of Hudibras, who says,

Has not the present parliament
A lodger to the devil sent,
Fully empowered to treat about
Finding revolted witches out?
And has he not within a year
Hanged threescore of them in one shire?

PETER, THE WILD BOY.

ON the continent of Europe, portions of which are interspersed with vast forests and uncultivated tracts, various individuals of the human species have, at different times, been discovered in a state no better than that of the brute creation. One of the most singular of these unfortunate creatures was Peter the Wild Boy, whose origin and history, previous to his discovery, must remain forever a secret. He was found in the year 1725, in the woods, about twenty-five miles from Hanover, in Germany. He walked on all fours, climbed trees like a squirrel, and fed on grass and moss.

When he was taken, he was about thirteen years old, and could not speak. He soon made his escape into the woods, where he concealed himself amid the branches of a tree, which was sawed down to recover him. He was brought over to England, in the year 1726, and exhibited to the king and many of the nobility. He received the title of Peter the Wild Boy, which name he ever afterwards retained.

He appeared to have scarcely any ideas, was uneasy at being obliged to wear clothes, and could not be induced to lie in a bed, but sat and slept in a corner of a room, whence it was conjectured that he used to sleep on a tree for security against wild beasts. He was committed to the care of Dr. Arbuthnot, at whose house he was to have been baptized; but, notwithstanding all the doctor's pains, he never could bring the wild youth to the use of speech, or the pronunciation of more than a very few words. As every effort to give him an education was found to be vain, he was placed with a farmer at a small distance from London, and a pension was allowed him by the king, which he enjoyed till his death, which occurred in 1785, at the age of about seventy-three years.

Peter was low of stature, and always wore his beard. He occasionally wandered away from his place of residence, but either returned or was brought back. He was never mischievous; was remarkable for his strength; became fond of finery and dress, and at last, was taught to love beer and gin. He was a lover of music, and acquired several tunes. He also became able to count as far as twenty, and could answer a few simple questions. He learned to eat the food of the family where he lived, but in his excursions, he subsisted upon raw herbage, berries and roots of young trees. He was evidently not an idiot, but seemed to continue in a state of mental infancy, thinking of little beyond his physical wants, and never being able to conceive of the existence of a God.

JOHN KELSEY.

It is well for every person to be apprized of the fact, that, in all ages and all countries, there are religious enthusiasts, who, having given themselves up to heated imaginations, lose the power of judging according to truth and reason upon this particular subject. They see things by a false vision, and are not only deluded but they often delude others. These persons are monomaniacs—insane upon the subject of religion, though often sane upon all others.

It appears that every person is liable to this species of delusion, if he gives up the reins to his fancy, and ceases to be guided by common sense; and the frequency of such occurrences shows that this liability is by no means remote. In a recent case, a man by the name of Elijah Thayer, a native of Massachusetts, conceived the idea that the present dispensation was speedily to pass away, and that the second coming of Christ was to be realized in his own person.

Believing himself to be commanded by God to announce this event to the great powers of England, Rome, and Jerusalem, he took passage in the steamer Britannia, in September, 1842, and proceeded upon his mission. He was a common laborer, but he possessed a good deal of knowledge, especially of the Bible. He was rational and sagacious upon all subjects except that of his peculiar religious views; and even in maintaining these, he displayed much skill, and was singularly dexterous in the quoting of Scripture.

Soon after his arrival, he proceeded to Windsor, where Queen Victoria was then residing. He made application for an interview with her majesty, saying that he had a most important communication to make to her. Being requested to state the substance of it, he sent her word that Elijah Thayer, the prophet of God, had come, by the command of the Most High, to announce a mighty change, which was speedily to take place throughout the universe. The present system of things was to pass away; crowns, thrones and sceptres were to be trampled in the dust; kings and queens were to be reduced to the level of common mortals; universal equality was to be established among mankind; an era of peace was to begin, and he himself, Elijah Thayer, passing from the prophetic to the kingly state, was to reign in righteousness over the earth as Christ himself.

This message was delivered by Elijah, in his fur cap, and his long-skirted blue coat, with a perfectly sober face, to the queen's servants at Windsor Castle. These received the extraordinary tidings with decorous politeness, promised faithfully to deliver the message, and the prophet, well satisfied, went his way. He now proceeded to London, and visited the several Jewish synagogues, announcing to the high priests his wonderful mission. The last we heard of him, he was preparing to make his way to Rome, in fulfilment of his insane project.

It would be easy to add numerous instances of similar delusion. In 1790, an Englishman, by the name of Richard Brothers, announced that he had a mission for the restoration of the Jews and to make Jerusalem the capital of the world. He said that he was commanded to notify the king, the lords and the commons of the same, which he did in a manner so obstreperous, that he was lodged in Newgate prison.

Roger North gives us an account of one John Kelsey, a Quaker, who, about the year 1680, "went on a sort of pilgrimage to Constantinople, for converting the Great Turk; and the first scene of his action was standing up in a corner of the street, and preaching to the people. They stared at him, and concluding him to be out of his wits, he was taken and carried to the madhouse; there he lay six months. At last, some of the keepers heard him speak the word *English,* and told of it so that it came to the ambassador, Lord Winchelsea's ear, that he had a subject in the madhouse.

"His lordship sent and had him at his house. The fellow stood before the ambassador, with a dirty, ragged hat on, and would not put it off, though he was so charged and admonished; thereupon the ambassador ordered him down, and had him drubbed upon the feet, after the Turkish manner. Then he was anything and would do anything, and afterwards did own that that drubbing had a great effect upon his spirit.

"Upon searching him, there was found in his pouch, among a few beans, a letter to the Grand Signior, very long and canting; but the substance was to let him know that he was the scourge in God's hand with which he chastised the wicked Christians; and now, their wickedness was so great, that God, by the spirit, had sent him, to let him know that he must come forthwith to scourge them.

"He was sent for England, but got off by the way, and came up a second time to Constantinople, from whence he was more surely conveyed; and some that knew John, told Sir Dudley North that they had seen him on the Exchange, where he recognised the admirable virtue of Turkish drubbing."

BAMFYLDE MOORE CAREW.

THIS eccentric character was born in 1693, at Bickley, in Devonshire, of which place his father was many years rector. Being descended from an ancient and honorable family, he was educated agreeably to his condition. At the age of twelve, he was sent to the Tiverton school, where his good behavior led his friends to hope that he might some day shine in the clerical profession. But the Tiverton scholars having at their command a fine pack of hounds, Carew, and two or three of his companions, devoted themselves more to hunting than study.

One day they engaged in the chase of a deer, just before the commencement of harvest. The animal took his course through the fields of grain, and the young sportsmen, with their hounds, followed, reckless of the damage that was done. The mischief was so considerable, that the proprietors complained to the school-master. Carew and his companions were so much frightened, that they absconded, and joined a gang of gipsies, who happened to be in the neighborhood. This society consisted of about eighteen persons of both sexes, who carried with them such an air of mirth and gaiety, that the youngsters were quite delighted with their company, and, expressing an inclination to enter into their society, the gipsies admitted them, after the performance of the requisite ceremonies and the administration of the customary oaths.

Young Carew was speedily initiated into all the arts of the wandering tribe, for which he seemed to have a happy genius. His parents, meanwhile, lamented him as one that was no more, for, though they had repeatedly advertised his name and person, they could not obtain the least intelligence of him. At length, after an interval of a year and a half, hearing of their grief and repeated inquiries after him, his heart relented, and he returned to Bickley. Being greatly disguised, both in dress and appearance, he was not known at first by his parents; but when he discovered himself, a scene followed which no words can describe, and there were great rejoicings, both in Bickley and the neighboring parish of Cadley.

Everything was done to render his home agreeable; but Carew had contracted such a fondness for the society of the gipsies, that, after various ineffectual struggles with the suggestions of filial piety, he once more eloped to his former connections, and soon gave new proofs of his aptitude for their peculiar calling.

Having remained with the gipsies for some time, he left them, and proceeded on a voyage to Newfoundland. He soon returned, and, landing at Newcastle, eloped with a young lady, the daughter of an eminent apothecary of that town. Proceeding to Bath, they were married, and paid a visit to Carew's uncle, a distinguished clergyman of Dorchester. He received them with great kindness, and endeavored to persuade his nephew to take a final leave of his gipsey life. This, however, proved vain, for Carew soon returned to that vagrant community, with whom he spent the remainder of his days.

He now led an adventurous career, seeming to be guided more by the humor of enterprise than the love of gain. His art in transforming his person so as to represent various characters, extorted from the gipsies themselves the greatest applause, and, at last, when Clause Patch, their king, died, Carew had the honor of being elected in his stead.

Though his character was known, he was rather a favorite with many persons of good standing, and was on one occasion invited to spend several days in hunting with Colonel Strangeways, at Milbury. The conversation happened one day, at dinner, to turn on Carew's ingenuity, and the colonel remarked that he would defy him to practise deception on him. The next day, while the colonel was out with his hounds, he met with a miserable object upon a pair of crutches, with a wound in his thigh, a coat of rags, and a venerable, pity-moving beard. His countenance expressed pain and sorrow, and as the colonel stopped to gaze upon him, the tears trickled down his silver beard. As the colonel was not proof against such an affecting sight, he threw him half a crown, and passed on. While he was at dinner, the miserable object came in, when lo, it was Carew himself!

The life of this singular man has afforded materials for a volume. His friends in vain offered to provide him with a respectable maintenance; no entreaty could prevail upon him to abandon the kind of life he had adopted. He spent about forty years with gipsies and beggars, and died in 1770, aged 77.

JOHN ELWES.

A MONOMANIAC is generally made by dwelling for a long period upon one object with intense interest, to the exclusion of others. By this process, this one object at last occupies the whole soul, fills the entire vision, and makes the mind blind to the relative importance of other things. A man in this condition is insane, and resembles the bedlamite, who, being asked why he was confined, replied, "I thought the world mad, and the world thought me mad, and they outvoted me!" While the world, guided by common sense, assigns to each subject its relative importance, the monomaniac we have imagined, sees but one thing, his own hobby, and pronounces mankind mad because they do not agree with him.

There are a thousand forms and shades of this insanity; one of the most common is displayed by the miser, who has dwelt so long and so intently upon the acquisition of money, that money becomes his idol: he thinks it the supreme good: he has a mad delight in amassing it: his eagerness to increase his store, quenches the lights of the soul—pity, benevolence, charity, and mercy; he is beset by a horrid fear of its being taken from him; and, as age creeps on and weakens his powers of body and mind, the demon of avarice takes possession of the bosom, and, putting out the light of reason, holds its revel in darkness and fear, till death closes the scene.

Of misers, history has furnished us a long list. We are told of M. Osterwald, a wealthy banker of Paris, who died in 1790, of want, yet leaving an estate of 600,000 dollars! When he began life, and bought a bottle of beer for his dinner, he took away the cork in his pocket. He practised this for a long period, and had at last collected such a quantity that they sold for nearly one hundred dollars! A few months before his death, he refused to buy meat for soup. "I should like the soup," said he, "well enough, but I do not want the meat. What, then, is to become of that?" The fear of losing the meat, led him to starve himself; yet, at the very moment, he had 800 assignats, of 200 dollars each, in a silken bag, around his neck!

Another Frenchman, by the name of Fortescue, affords a curious piece of history. He was a farmer-general of the taxes, and amassed an immense fortune by grinding the poor. The government at length called upon him for a considerable sum, but he pleaded poverty. Fearing that some of his neighbors should testify to his wealth, he determined to conceal it. He therefore dug a vault beneath his wine-cellar, where he deposited his gold. He went down to it by a ladder, and fastened the door by a spring lock. One day, while he was in the vault, the door closed, and the lock fastened him in! In vain were his cries for help! There he remained, till, worn out by horror of mind and starvation of body, he perished in the very midst of his heaps of gold! His miserable fate was not known till some years after, when, his house being sold, his bones were discovered in the vault with his treasures.

The celebrated John Elwes, whose portrait we have placed at the head of this article, has furnished a memorable instance of the inconsistency of man. He has showed that the most sordid parsimony may be combined with the greatest negligence and profusion, and that principles of the purest honor may be associated with a degree of meanness, that is utterly degrading to the human character. He was born in London, about the year 1714, his father's name being Meggot. He was educated at Westminster school, and afterwards went to Geneva, where he seems to have led rather a gay life.

On his return to England, his father being dead, he went to live with his uncle, Sir Harvey Elwes, a wealthy miser, who resided at Stoke, in Suffolk. In order to make a favorable impression upon his uncle, the nephew doffed his gay attire, at the little inn at Chelmsford, and appeared at Stoke with an old worn-out coat, a tattered waistcoat, darned worsted stockings, and small iron buckles in his shoes. He was received by Sir Harvey with satisfaction, who now adopted him as his heir. Here the two lived together, shivering with a single stick on the fire, occasionally dividing a glass of wine between them, and railing against the extravagance of the times. When night approached, they went to bed, to save the expense of candles!

But at last, Sir Harvey paid the debt of nature, and left his fortune, of more than a million of dollars, to his nephew. John Meggot, who was now about forty years old, adopted his uncle's surname agreeably to the will, and, while he inherited Sir Harvey's parsimony, he still addicted himself to gambling. He became a member of various clubs in London, and often played for very high sums. He once played two days and a night without intermission, the Duke of Northumberland being one of the party; and, as it was the custom among these gamblers in high life to throw aside the cards after being once used—at the close of the sitting, the party were nearly up to their knees in cards.

While Elwes was thus engaged, he had the most grasping desire of money, and, having sat up all night at play with persons of the highest rank, he would walk out at four o'clock in the morning, to Smithfield, to meet his cattle coming to market from his estates in Essex. There, forgetting the scenes he had just left, he would stand in the cold or rain, higgling with the butcher for a shilling. Sometimes, if the beasts had not arrived, he would walk on in the mire to meet them; and more than once he has gone on foot the whole way to his farm, which was seventeen miles from London, without stopping, after sitting up all night.

Mr. Elwes usually resided at Meacham, in Berkshire. In travelling between this place and London, he used to put two or three eggs, boiled hard, with a few crusts of bread, into his great-coat pocket; then, mounting one of his hunters, he would set off, taking the route with the fewest turnpike gates. Avoiding the taverns, he would stop under a hedge, and, while he ate his frugal meal, the horse would refresh himself by nibbling the grass.

Notwithstanding this excessive meanness, Mr. Elwes displayed many instances of generosity. On one occasion, he lent Lord Abington £7000, at a very critical moment, and entirely unsolicited, and when he had little reason to suppose the money would ever be repaid. Beside, he made it a principle never to ask for money which he won at play, and thus he lost many thousands of pounds, which he might have received by demanding it. At the same time, he had an equanimity of temper which nothing could disturb, and a gentleness and urbanity of manner, which never forsook him.

When he was somewhat advanced in life, he dismissed his fox-hounds, retrenched his expenses, and lived in the most parsimonious manner. Riches now rolled in upon him like a torrent; at the same time, his mean, miserly propensities increased. When in London, he would walk home in the rain, rather than pay a shilling for a coach; and sit in his wet clothes, rather than have a fire to dry them. On one occasion, he wore a black wig above a fortnight, which he picked out of a rut in a lane, and which had probably been discarded by a beggar. While the black, stray wig was thus atop of his own gray hair, he one day tore his coat, and, in order to supply himself, resorted to an old chest of Sir Jervaise, his uncle's father. From this, he took the first he came to, which was a full-dress, green, velvet coat, with slashed sleeves. In this attire, he sat down to dinner: not even the solemn severity of his poor old servant could resist the ludicrous effect of his appearance.

In order to invest his immense property, Mr. Elwes erected a great number of buildings in London, particularly about the Hay-Market. He was the founder of a large part of Mary-le-bone, Portman Place, Portman Square, and several of the adjacent streets. It was his custom in town, to occupy any one of his numerous houses that was vacant. Two beds, two chairs, a table and an old woman, comprised all his furniture. Thus he travelled from street to street, and it was often difficult to find him.

One day, his nephew, Colonel Timms, came to town, and, wishing very much to see him, made a long, but ineffectual search for him. At last, he was directed to a particular house, which he found, and knocked loudly at the door, but no answer was returned. He then entered, but all was silent below. On ascending to one of the chambers, he found Mr. Elwes on a shabby pallet bed, in a state of insensibility. The poor old woman, the partner of his journeys, was found lifeless on a rug in one of the garrets, where she had apparently been dead for at least two days, and where she had probably expired for want of the comforts of life. Mr. Elwes, being restored by cordials, stated that he had been sick for a long time, and wondered that the old woman did not come to his assistance.

Notwithstanding the unfavorable traits in Mr. Elwes' character, yet such was the confidence reposed in his integrity, that, without his own solicitation, he was elected a member of the House of Commons, for Berkshire, which he represented for three successive parliaments. Nothing could exceed the rigid fidelity with which he fulfilled his duties here. His vote was always given according to his conscience, and, in all weathers, and during the latest sittings, he was in his seat.

One night, as he was returning from the House of Commons, it being extremely dark, he ran against the pole of a sedan chair, and cut both his legs very badly. As usual, he refused to have medical assistance, but Colonel Timms insisted upon some one being called in. At length he submitted, and a surgeon was sent for, who immediately began to expatiate on the ill consequences of breaking the skin, the good fortune of his being sent for, and the peculiarly bad appearance of the wounds. "Very probable," replied Mr. Elwes, "but, Mr. ———, I have one thing to say to you. In my opinion my legs are not much hurt; now you think they are; so I will make this agreement. I will take one leg, and you shall take the other; you shall do what you please with yours; I will do nothing to mine; and I will wager your bill that my leg gets well before yours." He exultingly beat the surgeon by a fortnight.

About the year 1785, Mr. Elwes paid a visit to his seat at Stoke, which he had not seen for some years. On his arrival, he complained of the expensive furniture of the rooms. To save fire, he would sit with a servant in the kitchen, or walk about the remains of a ruinous greenhouse. During harvest, he amused himself with gleaning the corn upon the grounds of his own tenants. In the autumn, he would pick up stray chips and carry them to the fire in his pocket. On one occasion, he was seen robbing a crow's nest for fuel. He denied himself the common necessaries of life: one day, he dined on a moor-fowl, which a rat had drawn out of a river, and, on another, he ate the undigested part of a pike, which was taken from the stomach of a larger fish, caught in a net.

At last, the powers of life began to decay, and, in the autumn of 1786, his memory entirely failed him. On the 18th of November he sank into a state of extreme debility; yet he lingered till the 26th, when he expired without a sigh, leaving property to the amount of four millions of dollars. More than half of this was bequeathed to his two natural sons; the rest, being entailed, was inherited by Colonel Timms. Such was John Elwes, a singular compound of parsimony and profusion, of generosity and meanness, of honesty and avarice, of virtue and vice.

BARON D'AGUILAR.

THIS strange character presents another remarkable instance of inconsistency; of avarice and liberality, of cruelty and kindness, of meanness and integrity, of misanthropy and benevolence. He was the son of a German Jew, who settled in London, and left him his title, and a large estate. In 1758, he was married to a lady whose fortune amounted to 150,000 pounds. In 1763, being left a widower, he married a few days after, another lady of fortune. Up to this time, he had lived in the highest style of fashion, but, owing to the loss of an estate in America, and domestic disagreements, he now suddenly withdrew from his family connections and the society of the gay world, and established himself at a farm-house in Islington. Here he professed to be a farmer; he stocked his yard with cattle, pigs, and poultry, yet he kept them in such a lean and miserable condition, that the place acquired the name of Starvation Farmyard.

Everything in his establishment was conducted on the meanest scale; yet D'Aguilar, at this very time, was a liberal patron of public institutions, and profuse in his charities. While his cattle were actually in the agonies of starvation, he was doing some kindly, yet secret act, to alleviate the distresses of the poor. His wife had been obliged to leave him, but, after a separation of twenty years, he called to see her, and a reconciliation took place. In a short time, however, his extreme rigor compelled her again to leave him, and, by the advice of friends, she instituted legal proceedings against him. In this suit she was successful, and he was compelled to make a liberal provision for her.

At last, he was taken severely ill, and a physician was sent for, but he would not permit him to see him. He was therefore obliged to prescribe from a report of his symptoms. His youngest daughter begged permission to see him, but the stern father refused. In March, 1802, he died, leaving a property estimated at a million of dollars. His diamonds alone were worth thirty thousand pounds!

THOMAS GUY.

THIS gentleman was bred a bookseller, and began trade in the city of London, with no more than two hundred pounds. By his industry and uncommon frugality, but more particularly by purchasing seamen's tickets in Queen Anne's wars, and by speculations in the South Sea stock, in the memorable year 1720, he amassed an immense fortune.

In proof of his penurious disposition, it is recorded of him that he invariably dined alone, and a soiled proof sheet, or an old newspaper, was his common substitute for a table-cloth. One winter evening, as he was sitting in his room, meditating over a handful of half-lighted embers confined within the narrow precincts of a brick stove, and without any candle, a person, who came to inquire for him, was introduced, and, after the first compliments were passed and the guest requested to take a seat, Mr. Guy lighted a farthing candle which lay on the table by him, and desired to know the purport of the gentleman's visit.

The stranger was the famous Vulture Hopkins, characterized by Pope in his satires. "I have been told," said Hopkins, "that you, sir, are better versed in the prudent and necessary art of saving than any man now living, and I therefore wait upon you for a lesson of frugality; an art in which I used to think I excelled, but I have been told by all who know you, that you are greatly my superior." "And is that all you are come about?" said Guy; "why, then, we can talk this matter over in the dark." So saying, he extinguished his new-lighted farthing candle. Struck with this instance of economy, Hopkins acknowledged that he was convinced of Guy's superior thrift, and took his leave.

The penuriousness of this singular man seemed, however, to have for its object the indulgence of a systematic benevolence. He was the founder of a celebrated institution called Guy's Hospital, which cost him nearly 100,000 dollars, and, at his death, he endowed it with a fund amounting to a million of dollars. Nor were his benefactions confined to this institution. He made provision for his poor relations, founded a hospital at Tamworth, and made various donations for benevolent and charitable objects. He died in 1724, at the age of 81 years, having never been married.

OLD PARR.

THE extreme limit of human life, and the art of attaining it, has attracted the attention of mankind in ancient as well as modern times. Cornaro, an Italian, who died at the age of one hundred and four years, in 1566, wrote several treatises on this subject, the purpose of which was to prove that sobriety of life is the great secret of longevity. He shows that in his own case he restored a constitution prostrated by indulgence, to health and vigor. One of his papers was written at the age of ninety-five, and is commended by Addison in the 195th paper of the Spectator.

Sir George Baker gives us the history of a remarkable restoration of a constitution broken down by indulgence, in the case of Thomas Wood, a miller of Essex, England. He had been long addicted to high living and the free use of fermented liquors, but, at the age of forty-five, finding himself overwhelmed with a complication of painful disorders, he set about changing his mode of life. He gradually became abstemious in his diet, and in 1765 he began to drink nothing but water. Finding himself one day better without taking any liquid, he at last took leave of drinking altogether, and from October, 1765, to the time when Sir George Baker's account was drawn up, in August, 1771, he had not tasted a drop of water, or any other liquid, except in one instance. During all this period his health seemed to improve, under the strict regimen he had adopted.

The oldest man of whom we have any account in modern times, was Henry Jenkins, who resided in Bolton, Yorkshire. The only history we have of him was given by Mrs. Saville, who conversed with him, and made inquiries respecting him of several aged persons in the vicinity. He was twelve years old at the time the battle of Flodden Field was fought, in 1513, and he died, December 8th, 1670. He was, therefore, 169 years old when he died.

Of the celebrated Thomas Parr, we have a more particular account, furnished by Taylor, the Waterman, or Water-poet, as he is usually called. This is entitled "The Olde, Olde, very Olde Man; or the Age and Long Life of Thomas Parr, &c." It appears that the Earl of Arundel, being in Thropshire, heard of Parr, who was then, 1635, one hundred and fifty-two years old. Being interested in this extraordinary case of longevity, the earl caused Parr to be brought to London, upon a litter borne by two horses. His daughter-in-law, named Lucy, attended him, and, "to cheer up the olde man, and make him merry, there was an antique-faced fellow, called Jacke, or John the Foole," of the party. Parr was taken to court, and presented to Charles I. He died in London soon after his arrival, and was buried in Westminster Abbey, 1635.

Whether Parr's long life was greatly lengthened beyond that of ordinary men by a peculiar mode of living, we have not the means of telling. It is probable that there was something peculiar in his constitution. His body was dissected after death, and all the organs were found in a perfect state. We are also informed by an eye-witness, that

> "From head to heel, his body had all over
> A quick-set, thick-set, nat'ral hairy cover."

We may here mention an instance of longevity attained by an individual who spent his whole life in London. This was Thomas Laugher, who was born in 1700. His father died at the age of 97, and his mother at the age of 108. Though he was a liquor dealer during the early part of his life, yet he drank only milk, water, coffee, and tea. After a severe fit of illness at the age of eighty, he had a fresh head of hair, and new nails, both on his fingers and toes. He had a son who died at the age of eighty, some years before him, whom he called "Poor Tommy," and who appeared much older than his father. Laugher was greatly respected for his gentle manners and uninterrupted cheerfulness. He died at the age of 107. We have placed a sketch of him at the head of this article.

O'BRIEN.

THAT men of extraordinary stature, called giants, have frequently existed, we know, but there is no good reason to believe that the general stature of man was ever different from what it now is. If men were either smaller or larger than they are, they would be ill proportioned to the condition of things around them; beside, those of extraordinary height have usually a feeble pulse, and short lives. Those greatly below the usual stature, generally die early. It is fair to infer from these facts, that the present average height of man is the permanent standard. Among the mummies of Egypt, or the ancient remains of mankind found in other countries, there appears to be no general deviation from the common height.

Of the individual instances of great stature, Patrick O'Brien, born in the county of Kinsale, Ireland, in 1761, affords a memorable instance. He was put to the trade of a bricklayer, but such was his height at eighteen, that he was taken to England, and shown as the Irish giant. At twenty-five he attained the height of eight feet and seven inches; and, though not well made, his bulk was proportioned to his height. He continued to exhibit himself for several years, when, having realized an independence, he retired to the vicinity of Epping forest, where he died, in 1806. He was peculiarly mild and gentle in his character and manners. His body was enclosed in a leaden coffin, 9 feet 2 inches long, and to prevent any attempt to disturb his remains, his grave, by his own direction, was sunk twelve feet in the solid rock.

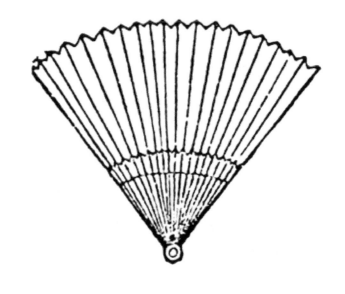

MAXAMILLIAN CHRISTOPHER MILLER.

THIS man was born at Leipsic, in 1694, and finally attained the height of eight feet. He travelled through Europe, being exhibited as a giant. He went to England in 1733, where he attracted attention by his great size, his enormous head and face, and his fantastic attire. His hand measured a foot, and his finger nine inches. He died in London, in 1734, aged 40.

HUYALAS.

IT was formerly said that the Patagonians were a race of giants, but it seems that they are but little larger than other races of men. South America appears to furnish its share of persons of extraordinary height. An instance is furnished in Basileo Huyalas, who was a native Indian of Peru, and was brought from the city of Ica to Lima, in May, 1792, to be exhibited on account of his enormous stature and extraordinary appearance.

His height was seven feet two inches and a half: his head, and the upper parts of his body, were monstrous. His arms were of such length as to touch his knees, when he stood erect. His whole weight was 360 pounds. At this period he was twenty-four years old. The annexed sketch gives a good idea of his appearance.

We are furnished with an account of a giant of New Grenada, an Indian, named Pedro Cano, who was seven feet five and a half inches high. His shoe was half a yard in length!

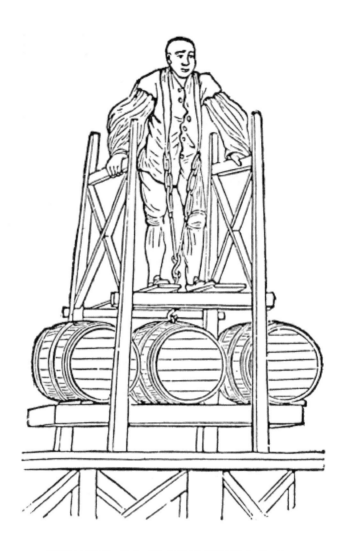

THOMAS TOPHAM.

THIS man, whose feats of strength might have figured with those of the heroes of Homer, was born in London, about the year 1710. He was bred a carpenter, and attained the height of five feet ten inches, being well proportioned in other respects. At the age of twenty-four, he took a tavern on the city road, and displayed his extraordinary powers in the gymnastic exhibitions then common at Moorfields. He was here accustomed to stop a horse by pulling against him, his feet being placed against a low wall. A table six feet long, with half a hundred weight upon it, he lifted with his teeth, and held it for some time in a horizontal position!

His fame for strength spread over the country, and his performances excited universal wonder. He would throw a horse over a turnpike gate, carry the beam of a house as a soldier his firelock, break a rope capable of sustaining twenty-two hundred weight, and bend a bar of iron an inch in diameter by striking it against his naked arm, into a bow! On one occasion, he found a watchman asleep in his box; he took them both on his shoulder, and carried them to the river, where he tipped them into the water. In May, 1741, he lifted three hogsheads of water, weighing 1836 pounds!

Though possessed of such wonderful strength, Topham was of a mild and pacific temper. His mind does not appear to have possessed the energy of his body, for, being deceived by a faithless woman, he resorted to the desperate resolution of taking his own life, and died by suicide in the flower of his age.

FOSTER POWELL.

THIS famous pedestrian was born near Leeds, in 1734. In 1762, he came to London, and articled himself to an attorney in the Temple. After the expiration of his clerkship, he was in the service of different persons, and in 1764, he walked fifty miles on the Bath road, in seven hours. He now visited several parts of Switzerland and France, where he gained much praise as a pedestrian. In 1773, he walked from London to York, and back again, upon a wager, a distance of 402 miles, in five days and eighteen hours. In 1778, he attempted to run two miles in ten minutes, but lost it by half a minute.

In 1787, he undertook to walk from Canterbury to London bridge and back again, in twenty-four hours, the distance being 112 miles, and he accomplished it, to the great astonishment of thousands of spectators. He performed many other extraordinary feats, and died in 1793. Though he had great opportunities of amassing money, he was careless of wealth, and died in indigent circumstances. His disposition was mild and gentle, and he had many friends.

JOSEPH CLARK.

In a work devoted to the curiosities of human nature, we must not omit Joseph Clark, of London, a man whose suppleness of body rendered him the wonder of his time. Though he was well made, and rather gross than thin, he could easily exhibit every species of deformity. The powers of his face were even more extraordinary than the flexibility of his body. He would suddenly transform himself so completely as not to be recognised by his familiar acquaintances. He could dislocate almost any of the joints of his body, and he often amused himself by imposing upon people in this way.

He once dislocated the vertebræ of his back and other parts of his body, in such a manner, that Molins, the famous surgeon, before whom he appeared as a patient, was shocked at the sight, and would not even attempt his cure. On one occasion, he ordered a coat of a tailor. When the latter measured him, he had an enormous hump on his left shoulder; when the coat came to be tried on, the hump was shifted to the right side! The tailor expressed great astonishment, begged a thousand pardons, and altered the coat as quickly as possible. When he again tried it on, the deformity appeared in the middle of his back!

Of the life of this remarkable person, we have few details, and we can only add that he died about the year 1700.

EDWARD BRIGHT.

THIS individual, who was remarkable for his great size, combined with active habits, was born in Essex, England, about the year 1720. He weighed 144 pounds at the age of twelve years. When he grew to manhood, he established himself as a grocer at Malden, about forty miles from London. He gradually increased in size, till he weighed nearly 500 pounds. He was still industrious and active in his mode of life, riding on horseback, and walking with ease. He paid close attention to his business, and went frequently to London to purchase goods.

At the age of twenty-three, he was married, and had five children. He was cheerful and good-natured, a kind husband, a tender father, a good master, and an honest man. When thirty years of age, he was taken with fever, and died, November 10th, 1750. At the period of his death he weighed 616 pounds.

DANIEL LAMBERT.

THIS individual was born at Leicester, England, in 1770, and was apprenticed to the business of a die sinker and engraver. He afterwards succeeded his father as keeper of the prison; and from this period, his size began to increase in a remarkable degree. In this situation he continued for some years, and so exemplary was his conduct, that when his office was taken away, in consequence of some new arrangements, he received an annuity of fifty pounds for life, as a mark of esteem, and the universal satisfaction he had given in the discharge of his duties.

His size increased to such a degree, that he was an object of universal wonder, and was at last persuaded to exhibit himself in London. Here he was visited by crowds of people, and, among the rest, by Count Boruwlaski, the Polish dwarf. The contrast between the two must have been striking indeed; for as Lambert was the largest man ever known, so the count was one of the smallest. The one weighed 739 pounds, and the other probably not over 60. Here were the two extremes of human stature.

In general, the health of Lambert was good, his sleep sound, his respiration free. His countenance was manly and intelligent; he possessed great information, much ready politeness, and conversed with ease and propriety. It is remarkable that he was an excellent singer, his voice being a melodious tenor, and his articulation clear and unembarrassed. He took several tours through the principal cities and towns of Great Britain, retaining his health and spirits till within a day of his death, which took place in June, 1809. His measure round the body was 9 feet 4 inches, and a suit of clothes cost him a hundred dollars!

JEFFREY HUDSON.

In the early ages of the world, when knowledge chiefly depends upon tradition, it is natural for mankind to people the universe with a thousand imaginary beings. Hence the stories of dragons, giants, and dwarfs, all of which have some foundation in reality; but when these are scrutinized, the dragon becomes only some wild beast of the forest, the giant is a man of uncommon size, and the dwarf of uncommon littleness.

We have already given some account of giants: we must say a few words in respect to dwarfs. These have never been known to be distinguished for their talents, though their figures are often perfectly well formed. They have generally one trait in common with children—a high opinion of their own little persons, and great vanity. In the middle ages, and even down to a much later period, dwarfs were a fashionable appendage to royal courts and the families of nobles.

Among the most celebrated of this class of persons was Jeffrey Hudson, born at Oakham, England, in 1619. At seven years of age, he was taken into the service of the Duke of Buckingham, being then but eighteen inches high. He afterwards was taken into the service of the queen of Charles I., who sent him to the continent on several confidential commissions. His size never exceeded three feet nine inches, but he possessed a good share of spirit, and, on the breaking out of the civil wars, he became a captain of horse.

On one occasion, he went to sea, and was taken by a Turkish corsair, and sold for a slave; but he was fortunately ransomed, and enabled to return to England. When the infamous Titus Oates pretended to reveal a plot against the king, Charles II., Hudson was one of the suspected persons, and, in consequence, lay some time in prison. He was at length released, and died in 1678.

JOSEPH BORUWLASKI.

THIS little personage was one of the most famous and agreeable of the pigmy race to which he belonged. He was a native of Poland, and, on account of his diminutive size, was early taken under the care of a lady of rank. She soon married, however, and he was transferred to the Countess Humieska, and accompanied her to her residence in Podolia. Here he remained for six months, and then attended the countess on a tour of pleasure through Germany and France. At Vienna, he was presented to the empress queen, Maria Theresa, being then fifteen years old. Her majesty was pleased to say that he was the most astonishing being she ever saw.

She took him into her lap, and asked him what he thought most curious and interesting at Vienna. "I have observed nothing," said the little count, smartly, "so wonderful as to see such a little man on the lap of so great a woman." This delighted the queen, and, taking a fine diamond from the finger of a child five or six years old, who was present, placed it on his finger. This child was Marie Antoinette, afterwards queen of France; and it may be easily imagined that Boruwlaski preserved the jewel, which was a very splendid one, with religious care.

From Vienna, they proceeded to Munich and other German cities, the little companion of the countess everywhere exciting the greatest interest and curiosity. At Luneville, they met with Bébé, a famous French dwarf. A friendship immediately commenced between the two little men, but Bébé was four inches the tallest, and Boruwlaski, being therefore the smaller of the two, was the greatest wonder. He was also remarkable for his amiable and cheerful manners. These things excited the jealousy of Bébé, and he determined to take revenge. One day, when they were alone, slily approaching his rival, he caught him by the waist, and endeavored to push him into the fire. Boruwlaski sustained himself against his adversary, till the servants, alarmed by the noise of the scuffle, came in and rescued him. Bébé was now chastised and disgraced with the king, his master, and soon after died of mortification and spleen.

The travellers now proceeded to Paris, where they passed more than a year, indulging in all the gaieties of that gay city. They were entertained by the royal family and the principal nobility. M. Bouret, renowned for his ambition and extravagance, gave a sumptuous entertainment in honor of Boruwlaski, at which all the table service, plates, knives and forks, were of a size suited to the guest. The chief dishes consisted of ortolans and other small game.

The countess and her charge returned to Warsaw, where they resided for many years. At twenty-five the count fell in love with a French actress, but she made sport of his passion, and his little heart was nearly broken. When he was forty years old, the black eyes of Isalina Barboutan, a domestic companion of the countess, again disturbed his peace; he declared his affection, but was again rejected. He, however, persevered, even against the injunctions of his patroness. She was so much offended with his obstinacy, that she ordered him to leave her house forever, and sent Isalina home to her parents.

He now applied to prince Casimir, and, through his recommendation, was taken under the patronage of the king. Continuing his addresses to Isalina Barboutan, he was accepted, and they were soon after married. By the recommendation of his friends, he set out in 1780 to exhibit himself in the principal cities in Europe. His wife accompanied him, and, about a year after their marriage, presented her husband with a daughter.

Passing through the great cities of Germany and France, the count arrived in London, where he was liberally patronized. He not only had exhibitions of his person, but he gave concerts which were well attended. In 1788, he wrote his life, which was published in an octavo volume, and was patronized by a long list of nobility. He at last acquired a competence, and retired to Durham with his family, where he spent the remainder of his days, and died at the age of nearly 100 years. He had several children, and lived happily with his wife, though it is said, that, in an interview with Daniel Lambert, he remarked that she used to set him on the mantel-piece, whenever he displeased her.

THE SIAMESE TWINS.

In the year 1829, Captain Coffin, of the American ship Sachem, arrived in the United States, with two youths, born in the kingdom of Siam, and united by a strong gristly ligature at the breast. Their names were Eng and Chang, and they were natives of Maklong, a village on the coast of Siam. They were born in May, 1811, of Chinese parents, who were in humble circumstances. They were engaged in fishing, keeping poultry, and manufacturing cocoa-nut oil, till they left their country. When they arrived, they were five feet two inches in height, well made, and muscular. They have been known to carry a person weighing 280 pounds.

The band that united these two persons was a cartilaginous substance, an eighth of an inch thick, and an inch and a half wide. It was flexible, and permitted the youths to turn in either direction. It was covered with skin, and seemed to be without pulsation. It was very strong, and of so little sensibility, that it might be smartly pulled, without seeming to give uneasiness. When touched in the centre, it was equally felt by both; but at half an inch from the centre, it was felt by only one.

They were agile, could walk or run with swiftness, and could swim well. Their intellectual powers were acute; they played at chess and draughts remarkably well, but never against each other. Their feelings were warm and affectionate, and their conduct amiable and well-regulated. They never entered into conversation with each other, beyond a simple remark made by one to the other, which seemed to be rationally accounted for by the fact, that, their experience being all in common, they had nothing to communicate. The attempt has frequently been made to engage them in separate conversations with different individuals, but always without success, as they are invariably inclined to direct their attention to the same thing at the same time.

In their movements perfect equanimity is observed; the one always concurring with the other, so that they appear as if actuated by a common mind. In their employments and amusements, they have never been known to utter an angry word towards each other. Whatever pleases or displeases one, has the same effect on the other. They feel hunger and thirst at the same time, and the quantity of food taken by them as nearly alike as possible. Both feel the desire to sleep simultaneously, and they always awake at the same moment. Upon the possibility of separating them with safety, there is some difference of opinion among medical men.

These two youths excited an extraordinary sensation upon their arrival in this country. For three or four years, they were exhibited here, and in Europe, and, finally, having obtained a competence, they purchased a farm in North Carolina, and established themselves as planters, where they still reside. They furnish the only instance in which two individuals have been thus united, and their case has probably excited more interest than any other freak of nature that has ever happened.

The most curious part of the story of Eng and Chang, is, that on the 13th of April, 1843, they were married to two sisters, Sarah and Adelaide Yeates, of Wilkes county, North Carolina!

Milton Keynes UK
Ingram Content Group UK Ltd.
UKHW051219151223
434437UK00016B/637